LONG CARRONADE

CANNON

SAMUEL CHESTER REID

*CAPTAIN OF THE AMERICAN PRIVATEER:
GENERAL ARMSTRONG*

A Naval Incident At HORTA

*AN AMERICAN PRIVATEER
VERSUS
A BRITISH NAVAL SQUADRON
IN THE WAR OF 1812*

*BY
PAUL
ESTRONZA
LA VIOLETTE*

A Naval Incident at Horta

Copyright 2011 by Paul Estronza La Violette

For reprint information contact:
laviolette@hughes.net

Published by Annabelle Books
707 Gray Station Road
Blairsville, Pennsylvania 15717
www.annabellebooks.com

All rights reserved. No part of this book may be reproduced or transmitted in any form or by any means, electronic or mechanical, including photocopying, recording, or by any information retrieval storage and retrieval system, without the written permission of the author.

Library of Congress Control Number: 2011901475

ISBN 0-9673936-6-3

987654321

First Edition

Front Cover
American Privateer *Grand Turk*
Built 1812, Wiscasset, Maine
309 tons, 14 guns, William Austin commander
Watercolor, signed: Ant Roux au Marseille, 1815
(Peabody Essex Museum)

Back Cover
Captain Samuel Chester Reid of the *General Armstrong*
(Oil by John Wesley Jarvis, 1815)

Contents

    A Few Words to Start…Pg. 15

Chapter 1
    The Arrival of the American Privateer, Noon, 26 September…Pg.23

Chapter 2
    The British Naval Squadron, 26 September…Pg. 39

    Interlude…Pg.55

Chapter 3
    Late Afternoon, 26 September …Pg.61

Chapter 4
    The First Action, Early Evening, 26 September…Pg. 77

Chapter 5
    Nine PM through Midnight, 26 September…Pg. 87

    A Few Notes on Guns…Pg.99

Chapter 6
    The Second Action, Midnight, 26 September…Pg. 107

Chapter 7
    Midnight through Dawn, 27 September…Pg. 129

Chapter 8
    The Third Action, the Scuttling and Burning of the *General Armstrong*, Dawn, 27 September…Pg. 139

Chapter 9
    Aftermath, 27 September - 5 October…Pg. 157

    Epilogue…Pg. 171

Contents (cont.)

Appendix A:
        Captain Reid's Report, and Captain Reid Afterward …Pg. 177

Appendix B:
        Commodore Lloyd's Report to Rear Admiral Brown and Commodore Lloyd and Commander Bentham Afterward …Pg. 189

Appendix C
        Letter from a British Observer Ashore…Pg. 195

Appendix D:
        Did the Battle of Fayal really lead to the Battle of New Orleans? …Pg. 201

Glossary…Pg. 210
Acknowledgements…Pg. 217

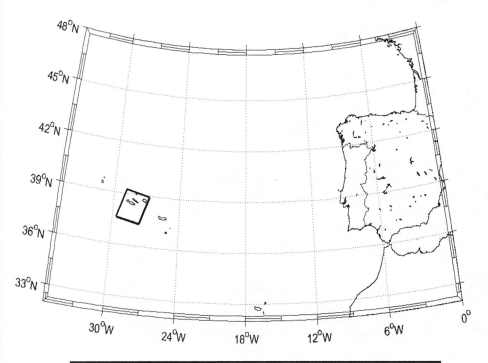

The Portuguese Azores (Or Western Islands)

    The Portuguese Azores (or Western Islands as it was often called in the 1800s) is a group of nine islands in the North Atlantic located approximately 1200 km west of Lisbon, Portugal, approximately 3,000 km east of Washington, D.C., and scattered over an area of approximately 1,000 km^2.

    Fayal (or Faial today) is the southernmost island in the center group of islands. The Bay of Horta and the principal town of Horta is located in the southeast corner of Fayal.

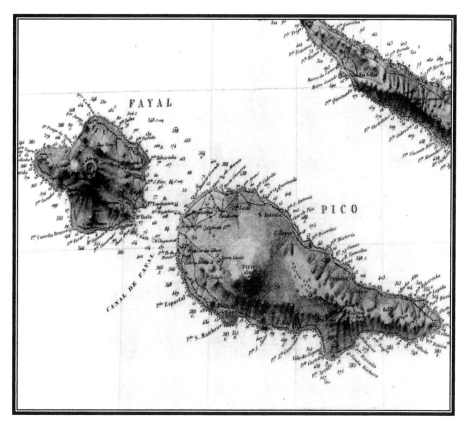

*Detail of an 1851 Portuguese chart,
(Portuguese Depot – General de la Marine)*

Other Books by Paul Estronza La Violette

Views from a Front Porch
Waiting for the White Pelican
Where the Blue Herons Dance
Sink or Be Sunk
A White Egret in the Shallows
Holly! and his Black Coat of Invisibility
One Dog, Two Dogs, Three Dogs, Four…
The Way to Stone Hill
Blueberry Peaches, Red Robin Pie (with Stella La Violette)

We anchored in the open roadstead of Horta, half a mile from the shore. The town has eight thousand to ten thousand inhabitants. Its snow-white houses nestle cozily in a sea of fresh green vegetation, and no village could look prettier or more attractive. It sits in the lap of an amphitheater of hills which are three hundred to seven hundred feet high, and carefully cultivated clear to their summits—not a foot of soil left idle. Every farm and every acre is cut up into little square enclosures by stone walls, whose duty it is to protect the growing products from the destructive gales that blow there. These hundreds of green squares, marked by their black lava walls, make the hills look like vast checkerboards.

Mark Twain, in *Innocents Abroad*, (1869) Chapter 5

(overleaf)

Horta Harbor, 1830. Forte de Santa Cruz and the landing mole associated with it are visible in mid shoreline of the bay.

Paul Estronza La Violette

A FEW WORDS TO START

*L*et me start by explaining a few things.

This book had its beginning in another book I wrote, *Sink or Be Sunk*, which also is about the War of 1812 and chiefly concerns the Battle of New Orleans. In that book, I concentrate on a series of naval actions that took place prior to the land battles with which most people are familiar. There is a final chapter in *Sink or Be Sunk,* which describes the land actions, but the remainder of the book details the little-known naval skirmishes that preceded these land actions.

In my five years of doing the research for *Sink or Be Sunk,* I was amazed at the lack of reliable data that was available. Although I found a great deal of material, I also found the details provided by these materials were often insufficient, contradictory, and, at times, unbelievable.

Even the statements of seemingly reliable contemporary witnesses often did not agree with each other. In writing my book, I often found myself having to make a choice on which of these materials I would accept as authoritative and which I would not.

What was even more disturbing was I often found reputable historians at times citing and using a contemporary witness's statement as fact when that statement was obviously in error.

The use of such an error can easily start a deadly sequence. If the individual historian is well thought of, he/she would be cited by others and the erroneous statement of what had happened will tumble endlessly through countless pages recounting incorrect history.

But, fortunately, there is another rich source of historical data.

This is the very dry, but surprisingly reliable, archival records, such as when a ship reported to a port or when supplies were sent some place and exactly where the supplies were stored. These may have errors as well, but, by their very nature, not as many.

I found myself, as I worked my way through very good and very bad information, relying on these mundane data sources for more and more details that not only fleshed out the immediate actions, but also gave accurate data as to why, where, and what took place.

What was more, these archival accounts often pointed to the correct path to take when I was faced with a choice of which of two seemingly accurate, but conflicting, authorities to believe.

In the end, based on my years of research experience as a naval oceanographer, I tried to present *Sink or Be Sunk* as a narrative detailing a long ago series of naval skirmishes. I tried to do this while staying as close as possible to what I believed actually happened.

In doing so, I based my narrative primarily on the several letters and reports of the men who were present during the engagement, despite the sometimes contradictions they had with one another.

I believe the book that resulted portrayed, as nearly as possible, what actually happened almost two hundred years ago. If nothing else, it made an exciting story.

Now, I am writing another book about the same period in our history, i.e., the build-up to the British attack on New Orleans.

In my writing I find myself again and again facing the same type of problem as I did in *Sink or Be Sunk*: what, in the small amount of personal accounts that are available, is the truth?

Most of what I write about in this book is based on the reports of the participants and witnesses' letters: the *General Armstrong's* commanding officer, Captain Samuel Chester Reid; the official reports of the Commodore of the British Squadron, Post-Captain Robert Lloyd; the American Consul, John Bass Dabney; the documents of the Portuguese Governor, Elias Jose Ribeiro; the ship and captain's logs of the British ships; and finally, both British and American observers on the shore.

Although, these accounts are an essential record of what happened, they often differ from one another; sometimes markedly. This is to be expected in the written accounts of the observers ashore, since they lacked the necessary knowledge of naval engagements to fully clarify what was taking place. It is not these that I have troubles with; it is the reports of the two commanders that stand unbelievably far apart.

In certain respects, this is understandable.

When one reviews the post-engagement reports of an armed encounter, such as detailed in this book, the two combatants wrote those reports for the review and influential opinions of their superiors or sponsors, rather than historians and readers, such as us who exist almost two hundred years in their future.

What, for example, Captain Lloyd stated happened at Horta might well shape the future direction of his career as a senior naval officer. Reid had a similar task in reporting to his sponsors. Perhaps an even harder task since he lost his ship in the Horta actions. Both men, therefore, colored the events in their reports to bolster their own motives.

Unfortunately, for the purposes of my writing about these events, the reports indicate that one of them did a great deal more coloring than the other.

In this book I strive to be as objective as possible with the information available and will, from time to time, give justice to all of the available accounts to let you be the judge of what did happen and what probably did not happen.

Finally, the historical perspective of the naval events described in this book has been enlarged by a number of writers of naval history as being the crucial pivot that decided the Battle of New Orleans.

These writers insist that if the delay created by the British naval involvement in Horta had not occurred, the British would have been able to conduct an earlier attack on an undefended New Orleans. General Andrew Jackson would not have been in New Orleans in time to set a defense of the city and no "Battle of New Orleans" would have taken place since the British would have already successfully attacked and occupied the city.

Hence the often-quoted remark:

If it weren't for the Battle of Fayal, there wouldn't have been a Battle of New Orleans.

Thus, we find a number of reliable historians writing that the British–American actions at Horta unhinged the tight schedule of the British invasion plan. The British, they say, went ahead with their invasion, but they went ahead late and found General Jackson waiting for them.

But is all this true? There is a great deal of evidence that indicates it is not.

In an effort to separate this controversy from interfering with the narrative of the Horta naval actions, I have attached a special appendix (Appendix D: Did the Battle of Fayal really lead to the Battle of New Orleans?) to allow the reader to judge if the statement attributed to General Jackson stands the examination of a later time.

In this book I tell the story from both the British and American's viewpoints.

To do this, you will find throughout the book the two sides designated by a separate motif: a long cannon for the Americans and a carronade for the British. When I shift from the American's view of the action, I precede that particular section with a long cannon, such as I have done here.

Conversely, when I shift the narrative to the British view of the action, I precede that particular section with the motif of a carronade, such as I have done here to the right.

In those chapters in which the British and Americans are fighting, I present at the start of the chapter both guns facing each other, muzzle to muzzle as shown below.

 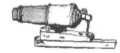

Finally, I believe the events I am about to describe tell a gripping story, a story of a naval battle that happened many years ago and a story about the brave and dedicated men who were engaged on both sides of that battle.

It's a good story.

As you read this, you will find that it is just that, a good story. I have tried to tell it as a story while staying as close as possible to what actually happened.

I hope you enjoy the account.

Paul Estronza La Violette
At Stone Hill,
Blairsville, PA
April 2011

Paul Estronza La Violette

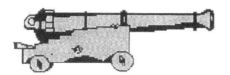 

4 JUNE 1812

THE UNITED STATES DECLARATION OF WAR

Be it enacted . . . , that war be and the same is hereby declared to exist between the United Kingdom of Great Britain and Ireland and the dependencies thereof, and the United States of America and their territories; and that the President of The United States is hereby authorized to use the whole land and naval force of the United States to carry the same into effect,

and to issue to private armed vessels of the United States commissions or letters of marque and general reprisal,

in such form as he shall think proper, and under the Seal of the United States, against the vessels, goods, and effects of the government of the said United Kingdom of Great Britain and Ireland, and the subjects thereof.

Paul Estronza La Violette

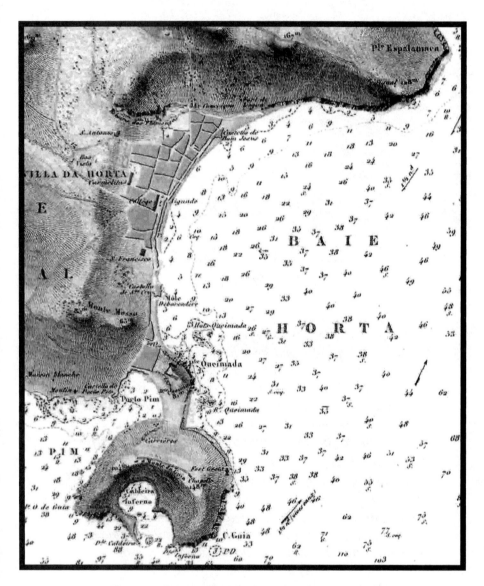

The Bay of Horta, Detail of an 1850 Portuguese Navigation chart
(Portuguese Depot – General de la Marine)

Chapter 1

THE ARRIVAL OF THE AMERICAN PRIVATEER, NOON, 26 SEPTEMBER

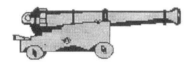

*I*t was noon and the brigantine standing in to the neutral Portuguese Port of Horta on 26 September 1814, was more than just an unusually pretty vessel.

She did indeed give any local observer with an eye to vessels of that era, a delightful, even sleek appearance. She had a long, dark hull and two tall, raked masts, seemingly overbalanced by immense square-rigged, bright white sails and an equally large fore-and-aft mainsail.

However, what would have attracted attention to the brigantine on this day in this port was the fact she flew a large American flag.

The Port of Horta was a way-station for vessels traversing the Atlantic from Europe to the Americas. As such, in normal times, the local population was accustomed to seeing such vessels coming and going in the port. Now, Great Britain and the United States were at war, and vessels, other than British, entering the port were a rarity.

Paul Estronza La Violette

The whole operation from the brigantine's approach and then her anchoring in the harbor, the last, while simultaneously dropping her gig on her starboard side as her anchor let go from the bow, was done prettily, as well. Even without seeing the broad American flag, the brisk manner of her doing these anchoring actions revealed her to be of Yankee origin.

Then, too, even the most inexperienced observers could tell by looking at her that the vessel was made for speed. They would be right in this, for the vessel was built for the sole and very deadly purpose of raiding British commerce and, as part of this effort, avoiding encounters with British warships. To do either of these actions, she had to be fast and, without a doubt, as hinted by her appearance, fast she was.

The vessel arriving in the neutral Port of Horta that September day was an American privateer operating under a letter of marque signed by the President of the United States, James Madison.

The vessel had had a quick passage to the Azores, departing New York in the late evening of 9 September, seventeen days earlier. She passed Sandy Hook in the extreme dark, coming close as she did so, to two warships of the blockading British fleet lying outside.

Despite the poor weather conditions and extremely poor visibility (that night having been chosen for her departure for exactly these conditions), the two large British warships, a 74-gun ship-of-the-line and a somewhat smaller razee, spotted the brigantine and the two carried on a chase that lasted through the long night and morning until, with a fresh favoring wind, the privateer left the two warships far behind.

A Naval Incident at Horta

The rest of the cruise could be considered uneventful except for one day's long, futile chase that ended with no prize and the privateer low on water, and on another day, a brief exchange of gunfire with a British brig that the brigantine readily outsailed.

It was her low water that resulted from her chase that caused the privateer to enter the Port of Horta and so she anchored in the bright, blue waters of the bay with a large flag identifying her as an American vessel and, while not quite as prominent, but still quite obvious to the attentive observer ashore, she had around her stern, in raised, large gold letters, the words:

General Armstrong, New York

As soon as the brigantine anchored, her commander, Captain Samuel Chester Reid, boarded his gig and had his coxswain point the small boat across the harbor to the long, stone mole jutting out on the south side of an old Portuguese fort.

It was a clear, beautifully calm day and the gig's crew pulling against a strong mid-ocean tidal current, soon closed the distance between the vessel and the shore and beached the gig between the mole and fort. Telling the men to wait, Reid headed to the long line of two-story, whitewashed buildings at the land end of the mole where a Portuguese flag identified one of the buildings as being the harbormaster's office.

Once inside the office, the harbormaster stood and greeted Reid. The room was large and the open windows exposed a broad view of the bay. Politely accepting the vessel's papers, the harbormaster motioned Reid to sit.

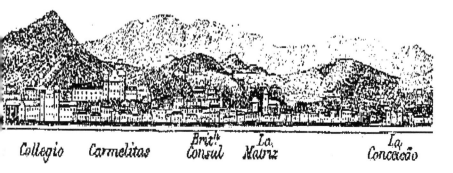

The harbormaster, in turn, sat behind a broad desk and except for occasionally asking a few questions in heavily accented English, began a long and intense examination of the *General Armstrong's* papers.

Minutes passed and, in the deep quiet of the room, Reid came slowly to realize from the stillness, that there was more involved in coming into this particular port and sitting here than just identifying himself and his vessel.

While Horta was a neutral port, he had thought there might be some difficulties. The Portuguese were trying to maintain their neutrality despite the fact that the port was often used by British war vessels operating in this area of the Atlantic. And here, complicating the port's neutrality, was a heavily armed, American privateer.

He sat, wet his lips, and waited.

As the harbormaster continued his seemingly endless shuffling of the vessel's papers, Reid turned and looked out the large window. The island of Pico, another of the islands in the Azores group, stood just four miles away. Nearby, sitting in the calm waters of the bay, lay the pride of his life, the *General Armstrong*. A small breeze brought the tangy smell of salt water into the room.

A crunching noise in the gravel outside indicated a carriage had pulled up. The harbormaster stopped his shuffling of the vessel's papers and, looking toward the door, smiled. The office door opened, and the two were joined by a pleasant-faced gentleman who, giving a warm greeting to the harbormaster, turned to Reid, shook his hand, and formally identified himself as the American Consul for the Azores, John Bass Dabney.

Dabney was a soft-spoken gentleman in his late forties who, as he talked, displayed the gentle mannerisms of the old school. His appearance in the harbormaster's office had an air of long-standing familiarity and, sitting at ease in an obviously accustomed place in a chair beside the harbormaster, he spoke with him in soft, familiar tones.

Finally, he turned to Reid and, with the harbormaster smiling near him, told Reid in a quiet voice that things had been arranged for his vessel to stay in port, at least temporarily. With this, the harbormaster stood, returned to Reid the *General Armstrong's* papers, bowed goodbye, and Reid and Dabney left the port office together.

Once outside, in the bright sun, Dabney was the very air of geniality. He invited Reid to join him in his carriage and to come up to the American Consulate to have a light lunch. After dining on monotonous ship's fare for two weeks, Reid gladly agreed.

The carriage moved along the cobbled street in front of the two- and three-storied whitewashed buildings bordering the waters of the bay; Dabney nodded to people, who, in turn, saluted him. It was obvious that he was a fixture in the town and, just as obvious by the actions of the locals that they passed, that he was well liked.

As they moved along the portside avenue, Dabney told Reid of his coming to the island at the turn of the century and falling in love with the island and its people. He had started a small import/export business mostly of wine. Once established he petitioned and won his present position as the United States Consul.

"You will like the wine, Captain Reid. I will give you a sample at lunch and, if it pleases you, I will have a case sent to your vessel to take with you when you leave. The wine comes from Pico, the rather pretty island you see across the channel. Unfortunately, for my purposes, Pico does not have a large harbor, so I have established my offices and do my business here in Horta."

Dabney went on to say that he had applied for the position as American Consul to help ease the official side of his business and, since his appointment by Thomas Jefferson in 1807, he had acted in that capacity. Until the present war, the synergetic melding of the business and the consulate had proven to work well.

But there was, unfortunately, the present war, and Dabney was familiar with the difficulties the Portuguese had in maintaining their neutrality. He had, he said, managed so far to get around many of the seemingly unsolvable problems that had evolved.

The ride along the waterfront promenade was not too long and rather relaxing. Soon they turned up one of the narrow, unbelievably steep, cobbled streets to what at its high end was *Bagatelle,* a beautiful house with large gardens that served as both Dabney's home and the offices of the American Consulate.

Bagatelle had been built by Dabney three years earlier and was justly his pride and joy. Sitting with some ices on a broad, bougainvillea-shaded veranda, among three acres of gardens, Reid allowed himself to relax.

The view of Pico's volcano was even grander from their higher elevation than it was at sea level. Below them, the *General Armstrong* sat, a child's toy floating peacefully as if in a broad, calm lake.

As they sat, Dabney explained in more detail the island's delicate and rather complex, diplomatic situation.

"American ships need special permission to stay in a neutral port such as Horta, especially an obviously heavily armed privateer such as yours. There are all sorts of rather complex rules. I'm sure you noticed the difficulty the harbormaster had when you dropped in seemingly out of the blue. Luckily, you were reported to me almost as soon as you dropped anchor.

"The difficulty rises from the fact that the British have developed a habit of using Horta as a rest-and-refurbishing station. In fact, I should tell you, two British brigs, *Thais* and *Calypso*, patrol this part of the Atlantic looking for privateers such as yours. What is worse, as far as you are concerned, is that these two vessels make a habit of using Horta as a logistical base for their several month-long patrols."

Dabney laughed when he saw the sudden change of expression on Reid's face.

A Naval Incident at Horta

Detail of an 1851 Portuguese chart. The mole on which Captain Reid came ashore is marked in the center with the Castele (Forte) de St. Cruze immediately above and to the left of it. (Portuguese Depot – General de la Marine)

"Please, excuse me. I didn't mean to scare you. I really wouldn't worry about them coming in while you are here. The last time *Thais* and *Calypso* were in port was when the British–French war ended this spring. The vessel's officers and men and the townspeople celebrated with a fiesta that lasted a week. I doubt if we will see those vessels again till mid-October.

"There was a British frigate, HMS *Rota,* that stopped for about a week awhile back. The ship's officers put on several plays. The playbill from one of them, 'The Tragedy of Barberossa,' I think, is around here somewhere. *Rota* left to form part of a British squadron sweeping the area north of here for privateers. When they left, they seemed to think they would be gone for some time.

"The point I am trying to make, Captain Reid, is that although the island depends on supplying vessels such as yours with needed supplies, the plain fact is few American ships come here.

"So this leaves the British warships as their biggest customers. When *Thais* and *Calypso* left, they paid a bill for their supplies and provisions of some 2,700 pounds sterling. That's quite a bit of money.

"Look at it, sir, from the Portuguese viewpoint. Since the United States and Great Britain are the only ones still at war here in the Atlantic and the local economy, already in dire straits, depends on any country's vessels stopping by for supplies, they have a touchy problem. A very touchy problem."

Dabney gestured, and a servant came from the house with a new serving of iced sherbet.

"They have tried to solve that problem by declaring Horta to be a neutral port," he continued. "So far it has worked. In fact, with the help of the Portuguese Governor, Elias Jose Ribeiro, and the British Vice Consul, Mr. Thomas Parkin, we have reached an amiable working agreement that so far has made it work well."

Reid nodded and then leaned forward.

"All I want, Mr. Dabney, is water. We need nothing else.

"We chased a schooner, on the eleventh. We caught up with her after a nine-hour chase and when we boarded her, we found she was a private armed American just six days from Philadelphia."

Reid paused, slightly embarrassed.

"It was a shame; we had scared the vessel's people so badly they had thrown over all her guns and, as it turned out, their water as well. It was an understandable mistake. We shared some of our water before we left them; it seemed the right thing to do. So, now we are the ones that need water. Hence our stop here in Horta.

"Once we receive the water we need, I assure you, sir, we will be happy to leave. Especially from what you have just now told me about those British warships."

Dabney nodded.

"Good, I thought you would not need to stay long and have already sent a request to the Portuguese Governor asking him to give you permission to be in port for a stay of twenty-four hours.

"If he grants my request, Captain Reid, and I am sure he will, you must leave by noon tomorrow. I have already arranged that you get all the water and whatever else you need before you sail. Yours will be a short stay, but I hope it will be a pleasant one."

They sat at the table for a little longer, looking out over the peaceful bay, the surrounding hills, and Pico's distant volcano.

Reid suddenly sat up. "Those British warships, you say they're brigs?"

"Why, yes they are."

"Well, I should say that the day after our meeting with the schooner, we had a brush with a British brig. It really wasn't much. She had the weather gauge on us, but we were too fast and we left her fairly easy in our wake."

Reid paused for a long moment, lost in thought.

"What we thought strange at the time, Mr. Dabney, was that they fired at us even though we were just out of range. It seemed an absurd thing to do, and we all had a good laugh about it.

"Then as a bit of a lark, we decided to return the compliment with a large gun we have aft. It's a 42-pounder that the men nicknamed "Long Tom." It's a perfect intimidator for stopping any arguments with a prize. The men love it. So we fired it. Although we were out of range of the brig, we felt the big splash the gun made when the big ball hit the water would entertain them."

Paul Estronza La Violette

(Above) Horta today, looking south. Forte de Santa Cruz, which forms a backdrop for much of the actions detailed here, is the long, dark structure at the far cusp of the harbor. The harbor has been changed since 1814. Land has been added in front of the fort and a large groin has been place in the harbor for loading and unloading ships. Monte da Guia, the immense, mound-shaped, volcanic feature at the southern part of Horta harbor, can also be seen in the 1870 picture of Bagatelle on the opposite page. (Picture by Zeorymer)

(Above) The veranda and front acreage of Bagatelle *as it was in the late 1870s. Today, the grounds are overgrown as to being almost impossible to walk. The house itself is in ruins with part of the roof falling in. (Classified Heritage of Faial)*

(Right) John Bass Dabney *(1767-1826) First American Consul to the Azores.*

He paused again, collecting his thoughts, going over again in his mind the brief affair and where he was now.

"I'm thinking that their firing may not have been just to impress us, sir; it may have also been to call attention to our being where we were to another vessel just over the horizon. The thing I am trying to say is that we didn't see anyone but the one brig, so we thought nothing of it at the time. But there may well have been another British brig.

"From what you tell me, our firing our big gun may have been a mistake. We exposed our having such a large gun when we didn't have to, to someone we did not really wish to know what we had."

Reid stopped for a second, plainly vexed.

"And now they know."

Dabney pursed his lips and nodded in agreement.

"It may well have been either the *Thais* or *Calypso*. They are brigs, after all, and neither one overly fast. Both have been on station so long they are past due for a dock work up.

"Now that you have brought that up, maybe it is good you won't be staying here any longer than tomorrow. They may well figure you will be heading here to water and are hurrying here, hoping to blockade you in port."

Dabney paused, calculating in his head.

"You say you saw the brig a few days ago?"

"Earlier than that, actually on the twelfth. But at the time, we were a goodly ways west of here. It may take them awhile. After all, we just got here."

"Good. Still, we must be careful. Given the differences in speed between you and them, and their perhaps thinking you may put in to Horta, they may well be standing in early the day after tomorrow looking for you.

"Luckily, you'll be long gone by then. It would, I assure you, create a very touchy situation for everyone. I'm not sure that if either of the brigs was to show, that Governor Ribeiro would not order you to leave the port immediately to maintain Horta's neutrality."

Reid looked at what was left of his iced sherbet. It had melted and with it the relaxed feeling he had enjoyed just a few moments earlier.

The cool taste of the ice and the grand view of Pico were gone. What was not gone, and was the more important to him, was his view of the vessel sitting below him in the quiet waters of the harbor. The possibility of being blockaded in Horta was not a pleasant prospect. But the other possibility, that of being forced to leave Horta and go out to fight one or maybe two British warships, with their highly trained crews and superior firepower, was even less appealing.

There was a small disturbance in the house, and a young man came out on the veranda and, bending low, spoke quietly to Dabney.

Dabney smiled and stood. "Captain Reid, this is my son, Charles. He has just returned from seeing the Governor and he tells me everything has been approved by the Portuguese authorities for your stay until noon tomorrow.

"Now, since you have been kind enough to invite me to come aboard the *General Armstrong* this evening, let me go about arranging your water, and I will join you for an early evening repast at about five."

He motioned to a servant.

"I will have the carriage take you back to the port and your gig. It will stay there, in case you need anything. Send it back with those needs, and I will see they are taken care of. Have a good day, sir, and I will see you on your vessel at five."

Dabney and his son exchanged bows with Reid, and Reid went out to the waiting carriage.

As the carriage carried him down the absurdly steep, cobbled road leading to the harbor, Reid mulled over the conversation he had just had.

He was not pleased with the way things were going.

Horta, despite its neutrality, now seemed too dangerous a harbor to stay in any longer than he had to.

***

What neither Reid nor Dabney knew was that a squadron of British warships was but a few hours outside the harbor of Horta, just a short distance to the north of the headland of the bay, Point Espalamca.

These were HMS *Plantagenet*, a ship-of-the-line with seventy-four guns; the frigate, HMS *Rota* (the same ship Dabney had mentioned to Reid during their lunch) with thirty-eight guns; and the brig, HMS *Carnation,* with eighteen guns.

These three ships were a part of Admiral William Brown's West Indies Command and, according to some reports, were returning to Nigel Bay, Jamaica to rejoin Admiral Brown's command for a special reason.

There are differing reports about that reason and why the squadron was where it was at this particular time. One fairly reliable report states that they were on an extended cruise sweeping the seas to the north and west for American privateers.

Several other reports state they were hurrying to return to their duty station, Jamaica, as they were scheduled to become part of a large British fleet being assembled in Jamaica under the command of Vice Admiral Sir Alexander Cochrane, commander of the North American Station. These same reports stress that the squadron was an integral part of the fleet's assembly and objectives.

Most importantly, these several accounts stress that the objective of the assemblage was an invasion of the southern United States, starting with the capture of New Orleans, and that the squadron of three warships were sorely needed for the success of that invasion.

These reports also stress that Post-Captain Robert Lloyd, the Commodore in command of the three warships, was under orders to proceed at all haste to Jamaica, that his orders were specific, and that the urgency of his mission was implicit in these orders.

If these reports were true, all of this would change in the next twelve hours.

"A Ship of War, of the Third Rate"
(*From* Cyclopaedia, *Volume 2, 1728*)

Chapter 2

THE BRITISH NAVAL SQUADRON

EARLY AFTERNOON, 26 SEPTEMBER

𝓗MS *Plantagenet,* moving through the sea just to the north of Point Espalamca, was a magnifcent ship, a beautiful paradigm of the period's ships-of-the-line.

Plantagenet was a third rate (the number of guns being the basis of the rating, not the condition of the ship itself). She was large: 181 feet long at the gundeck with a beam of forty-seven feet. Built in 1801 at Woolwich, England, she was designed by Sir William Rule as one of Great Britain's large class 74s.

As befitting a ship-of-the-line, *Plantagenet* was well armed. She carried two full decks of long guns. A full broadside from *Plantagenet* threw almost a half ton of iron at an enemy ship. She was equally well manned; almost six hundred men formed her crew with more than a hundred of these being marines

Ships-of-the-line, such as the *Plantagenet*, were the battleships of the 18th and early 19th century British navy and formed the backbone of the basic naval battle engagement strategy of the period.

In the naval actions of that time, *Plantagenet* would be part of a *line of battle* composed of similar vessels (hence the name, ship-of-the-line). These would maneuver in a tightly choreographed line parallel to a similar line of enemy ships-of-the-line. Once in position, the two lines would pound each other until one or the other protagonists won.

It was a plan of battle that would become hopelessly outdated within two decades of the actions described here. However, it was the basic naval tactic of the time and so was used by all commanders of ships-of-the-line at their peril.

In fact, Admiral the honorable John Byng was court marshaled and shot by a firing squad in 1757 for not explicitly following the British navy's tightly scripted "Fighting Instructions" for fighting in such a line of battle.

However, Admiral Horatio Nelson did win battles following battle tactics dictated by the "Fighting Instructions" in his action in the Battle of the Nile (although he did deviate to some extent in the Battle of Trafalgar).

Due to the importance of ships-of-the-line, commanding officers of such ships were, in theory at least, the best the British naval method of vetting officers could produce. The commanding officer of the *Plantagenet* should, from this reasoning, be the best of many.

In the actions that are about to take place in the Port of Horta, this theory will be sorely tested.

Plantagenet, as grand as she was, had a bit extra to add to her imposing presence. She flew a broad, swallow-tailed pennant, signifying she carried aboard a Commodore, i.e., a flag rank officer in charge of a squadron of British warships.

The rank of Commodore was a temporary one, held only as long as the squadron sailed as a group under a single command. But it was a flag-rank position and, despite it being temporary, it represented a great deal of power.

The squadron Commodore on board *Plantagenet* was Post-Captain Robert Lloyd. He had been captain of *Plantagenet* before his temporary appointment to Commodore. What was unusual in this case was that while acting as Commodore, Lloyd did not relinquish direct control of *Plantagenet,* that is, delegate a flag captain to run the day-to-day actions of the ship.

Lloyd had seen a great deal of action that had helped his attaining his Post-Captaincy. Much of this had involved the successful capture of enemy privateers. He was very aggressive in these encounters and, as a result, had received several rather serious wounds, one that involved an injury to the head by a half-pike.

The *London Gazette* had lauded his exploits. One *Gazette* article reported that between 8 September and 17 December 1813, Lloyd had taken no less than twenty privateers and commercial sails, measuring a total of 1,200 tons.

By any measure, this was a goodly amount of prizes.

During this early period, he had the command of several smaller warships, the frigate, HMS *Guerriere*, (1809) being the most notable for our purposes. After a short time on HMS *Swiftsure,* a 74 (1810), and subsequently, ten month's ashore on half pay, he was appointed *Plantagenet's* commanding officer when she first arrived in American waters in 1812.

His earlier command of *Guerriere* has certain significance in the Port of Horta actions, as we shall soon see. He seems to have had a parental interest in this ship, as he appears to also have with *Plantagenet*.

Guerriere, under a captain posted to the ship some time after Captain Lloyd's departure, became a *cause célèbre* in the Great Britain-American war when she lost a battle to the USS *Constitution.*

The fact is the USS *Constitution*/HMS *Guerriere* affair was a decisive battle that, by its outcome, established, without question to much of the world's naval powers, the fighting ability of the fledgling American navy.

It was high praise, especially since it was a navy that had no ships-of-the-line. Instead, it had as its top warships, a fleet of six frigates, such as the *Constitution*, some of which were still being built during the War of 1812.

In the actions that take place over the next two days, Lloyd's earlier command of *Guerriere* and the fact that the *Guerriere* was later lost in battle to the *Constitution,* appears to play bitter in Captain Lloyd's mind.

There is little material available about Post-Captain Robert Lloyd as a person, except that a close look at the list of his past prizes shows that he did seem to have a deep abiding dislike of privateers.

He appears to have been a strict disciplinarian, a good sailor, and a British naval officer who would, if everything worked well in the normal course of seniority succession, ascend, with time, to an admiral's flag. His command of the *Plantagenet* and now Commodore of a squadron of British warships was a normal step in this advancement.

From what is known about him, it is obvious he had a temper, a domineering mannerism and, unfortunately, he, like many senior British naval officers in the years following the American Revolution, had a deep disdain for the fighting abilities of Americans.

If the *Constitution's* battle with *Guerriere* had started to change that opinion on the world's stage, it had not changed Captain Lloyd's. To him, it did not seem possible that an American ship could win a sea battle with a British ship. That obviously just could not happen.

The fact is that to Captain Lloyd, *Constitution's* win over the *Guerriere*, like the winning of the thirteen colonies' freedom from Great Britain twenty-one years earlier, had been a fluke that begged correcting by a force of arms, preferably British arms.

To Lloyd, as to many of his fellow British naval officers, the present war was an opportunity to do that correcting.

A Naval Incident at Horta

The USS Constitution *vs. HMS* Guerriere, *oil by G. T. Margeson
(Navy History and Heritage Command)*

There were two other ships in the *Plantagenet's* entourage. These were the 38-gun frigate, HMS *Rota,* and the 18-gun brig sloop, HMS *Carnation.*

Rota, under the command of Post-Captain Philip Somerville, was a good example of the warships that were becoming the workhorses of the British navy. In all the actions that concerned American ships in the War of 1812, British frigates and lesser vessels were the warships that the Americans engaged in combat.

In the American campaigns, the importance of Great Britain's ships-of-the-line played a comparatively minor role. In fact, many ships-of-the-line were being modified to the changing methods of naval warfare that the American campaigns brought about. The razee that chased Captain Reid when he rounded Sandy Hook was actually a former ship-of-the-line that had been reduced in height by the removal of her upper deck, making her more manageable in action.

Although ships-of-the-line, such as *Plantagenet*, helped maintain the blockade of American ports, it was essentially frigates that became engaged in the several high-profile American/British naval battles.

An interesting point concerning *Rota* and essential to the understanding of the series of actions that are about to take place in Horta, is that *Rota* was a prize. She had been a Dutch frigate before her capture in the 1801 Battle of Copenhagen.

The remaining and smallest vessel in the squadron, the 18-gun brig sloop HMS *Carnation*, had been built in England in 1813.

Carnation followed the much proven British design of the *Cruizer*-type brig, the most numerous class of warships built by the British navy during the long years of the Napoleonic Wars. All told, there were 181 of this class in service in the British navy in 1814.

HMS Polorus, *a Cruizer-class brig sloop (water color, artist unknown)*

    Thais and *Calypso,* mentioned in the earlier discussions of Dabney and Reid on the veranda of *Bagatelle,* were *Cruizer*-class brigs.

    Carnation carried 32- and 12- pounder carronades as her main armament of guns rather than long cannon. These powerful guns, called "smashers" by many of their advocates, were being carried by more and more British warships. Their biggest limitation was that their range was half that of the standard long cannon then in use.

Veteran British naval officers had strongly resisted the introduction of carronades being made part of the main armament of warships larger than brigs (in fact, *Plantagenet* had a number of carronades, but did not count them as part of her seventy-four long cannon).

In addition to her main battery of carronades, *Carnation* carried two long cannon (6-pounders) in her bow to be used as "chasers." These bow-mounted cannon were normal armament to brigs and frigates. They gave these ships the distant firing range they needed when chasing an enemy ship. It was probably a bow chaser that was used by the brig that exchanged gunfire with *General Armstrong* prior to her arrival at Horta.

(Since the difference between carronades and long cannon is important in the actions that take place in Horta, a more detailed discussion on the pros and cons of the two will be made in Chapter 5.)

Carnation sailed under the command of Commander George Bentham. Although addressed as captain as a courtesy of his command, his official rank was actually Commander, a naval rank below Post-Captain or the equivalent to a Major in the army.

Whereas, a Post-Captain's advancement went strictly by seniority, a Commander's advancement to the next step in rank, i.e., Post-Captain, depended a great deal on his actions as Commander. Bentham's skill in commanding the *Carnation* would be severely tested in the following actions.

***

There is still an hour before the Portuguese pilot will come aboard *Plantagenet* to guide the squadron into the bay. The pilot's conversation with the *Plantagenet* officers and a letter from the British Vice Consul will start a chain of circumstances that will markedly change the ability of the British squadron to continue on its present cruise.

Let us take the time before this happens to explain a system used by the British Admiralty during the period of which we are talking. It is basically a system to encourage the maximum efforts of officers in the British naval service and it appears to have worked quite well.

This is the awarding of *prize money*.

Captured ships during the late 1700 and 1800s instantly became Crown property to be sold into the British merchant service or reused as men-of-war. Such sales were a valuable source to the Crown in both money and new ships for the navy.

Not all of the money from these sales was kept by the Crown; some was doled out as an enticement to garner more prizes. A good portion was meted to the Admirals and their aides, to the vessel captains involved in the actual action, to the ship's officers, and to a far lesser extent to the ship's crews involved in the action.

Thus, the prize money was in essence a tangible reward that inspired the efforts of British officers to both do battle with the enemy and to remain at sea for long periods looking for prizes. As a result, there were many rich naval officers, especially flag officers, since they garnered the greatest share of a prize award.

What was most expedient, as far as the Treasury of Great Britain was concerned, was that all of this was accomplished at almost no cost to the Crown. It was, in effect, a win-win method of waging naval warfare.

The prize money doled out to the capturing parties of enemy ships came from the sale of the captured vessels and their cargos. If the prize was, for example, an enemy warship and repairable, the Crown bought it for its own use as a naval vessel and added it to the fleet.

As just mentioned, *Rota* was such a capture, and the British officers involved in her capture shared in the prize money. As she was repairable at the time of her seizure, she was refitted and commissioned as a British man-of-war.

This practice of doling out prize money to the men responsible for the capture of enemy vessels had a strong influence on the way the British navy fought its battles.

While all this had strong advantages to the British navy's success and reputation, there was a serious drawback. Boarding an enemy vessel and the hand-to-hand fighting with its high casualty rate remained a common tactic long after naval guns, capable of sinking an enemy vessel at a distance, were developed.

In essence, the practice of prize money encouraged the capture of enemy vessels rather than their sinking. This fact is to be noted as it plays an important role in the events about to take place in the Bay of Horta.

***

With this said, let us return to the *Plantagenet* and her entourage as they are about to enter the neutral Portuguese port of Horta.

Captain Lloyd's cabin was rather impressive in its fine details. *Plantagenet* was, after all, a ship of war, but some effort had been made in the captain's large cabin's decor to soften this lethal stance.

The two large, 24-pound, side cannon and a huge, 32-pound stern chaser required for the ship's battle duties were in the cabin. However, these were enclosed in quaintly painted cupboard-like enclosures so that to a naive visitor, their presence was not obvious.

Although the overhead was low, the cabin was spacious, stretching across the entire ship. Massive beams extended from one side of the broad room to the other in extraordinarily long, beautiful curves. The canvas covering the wooden deck was in turn covered by several large, rather expensive rugs on which sat several pieces of comfortable furniture: a small table, several comfortable chairs, a large desk, and attendant cabinets.

All of the accouterments of this cabin could be swept away in seconds when the ship's company was beat to quarters, and the large, comfortable room would, in a matter of moments, be filled with sweaty men readying the now suddenly exposed large guns into what they were meant to be: mechanisms of destruction.

The best features of the large cabin lay in its several sets of multi-paned windows slanted down from the overhang. The windows ran from one side of the ship to the other and presented to the room's occupants a splendid view of the broad sea behind *Plantagenet.*

At the time we are speaking about, the grand view through the windows contained *Rota* following dutifully in the flagship's wake. The handsome frigate was bathed in the light of the afternoon sun, a sun which, in turn, flooded the large cabin with a soft, almost golden, light.

Carnation was not in view as she normally would have been; that is as another rigorously aligned ship sailing behind *Rota* in rigid column behind the flag. She had been deployed to act as observer and scout to the east of the squadron. On her return, she had been instructed to proceed ahead of the others into Horta harbor.

The luxury of the cabin's broad space and large stern windows was much as was commonly found in all ships-of-the-line and one that justifiably befitted a senior Post-Captain or Commodore of the British navy. It was certainly larger than the cabin the present resident had when he had been in command of the *Guerriere* or that Commander Bentham enjoyed on the *Carnation.*

If there was one sole element that might be used to reflect the elevated status of a senior Post-Captain's rank and command, it was this cabin and its splendid view.

It was, however, a double-edged sword. If it impressed visitors with the implied power of its tenant, it also bestowed upon that same tenet a feeling of that power that was hard for a lesser person to ignore. Unfortunately, Captain Lloyd did not appear to be not immune to such feeling.

49

As we return to our story, Captain Lloyd sits at his desk in the room working over several of the sea of documents required by his command. There is a knock on the cabin door and with his brusque reply to enter, the open door reveals in the narrow passage immediately outside, the ubiquitous marine guard and the form and conscientious face of his first lieutenant.

Following a perfunctory wave from Lloyd, the lieutenant entered the room and stood attentively in front of his captain's cluttered desk. There was a long moment. The lieutenant remained standing.

Finally, Lloyd scratched his signature to several of the documents in front of him and placing his pen carefully in its holder, looked up and nodded to his First.

The lieutenant murmured, "Commodore," and handed Lloyd a white envelope. "When the harbor pilot came aboard, sir, he brought with him this note from our Vice Consul ashore, Mr. Parkin."

As Lloyd took the letter, his First added a few words of information.

"Sir, I thought you might be also interested in some news the pilot brought with him. It concerns a visitor that came into port about noon today and is now anchored opposite the old fort."

The First paused for effect and then continued.

"He says, sir, that it's an American privateer."

Lloyd stopped opening the consul's letter and looked up at his first lieutenant.

"What? An American pirate in the harbor! I thought Horta was a neutral port. This is unbelievable! What type vessel is it?"

The First smiled.

"The pilot says she is a brigantine, sir. He also says she is rather well handled and, from her looks and large spread of sail, appears to be very fast."

Lloyd looked at his first lieutenant, absorbing what he had said, and then finished opening the note from the British Vice Consul.

It wasn't a long note, but Lloyd read it twice, then a third time. Finally, he placed it on his desk and looked up once again at his First. His voice was now quiet, reflective.

"Mr. Parkin agrees with the pilot. He states the vessel is an American privateer, the *General Armstrong*. However, there is more. He informs me the Portuguese governor has given her until noon tomorrow to stay in port. Then, of course, she must leave. Mr. Parkin particularly asks our forbearance during her overnight stay."

With this, Lloyd stared again at the note in abstract thought. After a long moment of silence, his first lieutenant began to speak.

"Perhaps *Rota* can stand outside in the channel, sir, and wait for the—"

Lloyd raised his hand to silence him. Then looking once again at the letter on the cluttered desk, he stood, slowly turned, and looked out the broad gallery of windows. The room became very quiet. The First stood stock still waiting.

Then Lloyd spoke, still staring out the window.

"You say the pilot said the brigantine appears to be fast?"

"Oh, yes, sir. Very fast. And, I should add, that he says she's a rather pretty thing, too."

A minute, then two minutes went by.

Finally making a decision, Lloyd turned back to his First and, sitting back down at his desk, began issuing a series of instructions.

"Signal *Carnation*…"

After his First left, Lloyd turned his chair and continued staring out the large rear windows.

Beyond the window, *Rota* still sailed in her rigorously maintained position, seemingly without wavering. Beyond, the frigate's wake stretched a straight line of white on the blue water.

The silence returned.

Then (actually only a few minutes after the departure of his First), Lloyd heard the screech of the boatswain's whistle and the pad of men's feet running on the deck above him. With this came a definite shift in the ship's movement.

All of these told him that *Plantagenet* had passed the headland and had turned in preparation to entering the bay.

Lloyd stood, called loudly for his valet, and began making preparations to go on deck.

The naval action in the Bay of Horta, for all intent and purpose, had begun.

A Naval Incident at Horta

THE ENDING AND START OF IT ALL

The painting, Surrender of Lord Cornwallis, *depicts the British surrendering to French and American forces after the Siege of Yorktown (28 September – 19 October 1781) at the end of the American Revolutionary War. (Oil by American artist John Trumbul, 1817. Now exhibited in the United States Capitol rotunda.)*

British disdain of the Americans at the surrender was obvious. Major General Charles Cornwallis actually refused to come to the surrender ceremony, claiming illness. Brigadier General Charles O'Hara initially presented the British sword to Comte de Rochambeau, who refused it and pointed to General Washington. When O'Hara offered it to Washington, he, in turn, motioned to his second-in-command, Benjamin Lincoln, who had been humiliated by the British at Charleston, to accept it.

The British soldiers marched out between the French and American armies, as, according to legend, the British drummers and fifers played "The World Turn'd Upside Down."

INTERLUDE

𝒯he animosity between British senior naval officers such as Lloyd against the American navy and privateers, or for that matter just about anything to do with the American military, had been brewing for years.

It wasn't just the Revolutionary War. Essentially it was about the way the Revolutionary War ended; it was a deep feeling that it was only the intervention by the French that allowed the fledgling United States to obtain its liberty. This had been a slap in the face to the British military.

A prime example of the British military mind at the time was personified by Admiral Cochrane, the admiral in charge of assembling the army and fleet to attack New Orleans. Firmly implanted in his mind and heavily reflected in his actions was the opinion that in waging war with Americans, he was "chastising undisciplined rabble."

But there was more than just the British military attitude in the early 1800s that led to the War of 1812. Other European countries besides Great Britain felt the United States had won its freedom by accident and did not warrant any due deference from the European nations.

There was an almost universal European attitude that treated the United States as if it was a third-rate country, easily pushed aside if it was expeditious to do so.

In the years following 1783, there were a series of confrontations which reflected this European view.

First, there was a problem when Spain tried to impose large taxes on cargoes coming down the Mississippi River and passing New Orleans. America was expanding to the west. The principal roadway for commerce produced west of the Allegany Mountains was the Mississippi River rather than eastern seaboard ports. Conflict was narrowly avoided when the tax was canceled.

But a bigger slap to the young nation was the Quasi-War with France. France had a revolution of its own in 1794. After the revolution, it was a very different nation than the friend that had helped the United States in its War of Independence. Great Britain and the new France were again at war and a trade deal between the Americans and the British led, in turn, to French outrage.

France began to seize American ships trading with Britain. This expanded with the French inflicting substantial losses on American shipping as French privateers cruised up and down the U.S. Atlantic seaboard. A 'Quasi-War' began in July 1798, and lasted until an agreement was reached to cease hostilities at the Convention of 1800.

And so it went.

The final insult in this long list of European insults, and one that almost by itself led directly to the British–American war, was the wanton stopping and boarding of American ships on the open ocean and impressing seamen from those ships.

The actual process of impressment started innocuously enough. Great Britain's war with Napoleon strained British naval resources. It desperately tried to maintain a blockade of almost the entire coast of Europe.

British warships began stopping American ships at sea to inspect them. This soon went beyond just examining ships' papers to examing the ship's crew and 'pressing' any of the men the boarding officer considered ex-British seamen.

Because of the blockade, most British naval ships were shorthanded and the stopping of American vessels became a prime source of fulfilling the British warships' complement of men. Soon their navy exploited this rich lode of manpower.

All of this came to a head on 22 June 1807.

Several British and American sailors had deserted British warships that had been blockading some French ships in Chesapeake Bay. These men had subsequently joined the crew of the American navy frigate USS *Chesapeake*, commanded by Captain James Barron.

In an attempt to recover the deserters, HMS *Leopard* overtook the *Chesapeake* at sea and requested permission to search her. Captain Barron refused, so *Leopard* opened fire, killing three crewmen, and wounding eighteen.

Caught completely unprepared, Barron surrendered. The British boarding party seized four deserters from the Royal Navy — three Americans and one British-born sailor — and took them to Halifax, where the British sailor, Jenkin Ratford, was later hanged for desertion.

The continuing insults, such as this, to the United States' sovereignty and the forcing of European nations to make the United States take sides in their incessant wars were, with this action, coming rapidly to a head.

The USS *Chesapeake*/HMS *Leopard* affair became a *cause célèbre* that became a rallying cry in the United States for war with Great Britain

In June 1812 the United States declared war on Great Britain. It was a bitter war that should have ended with the treaty signed in Ghent in December 1814.

However, Admiral Cochrane and General Andrew Jackson did not receive word of the signing of this treaty until after the Battle of New Orleans.

This was just as well.

There was more to acceptance of the Treaty of Ghent than what was originally written in the text of the treaty. There were the results of the Battle of New Orleans.

General Andrew Jackson, in a series of land actions that began in December 1814 and ended in January 1815, severely beat a British army composed of what was considered 'Wellington's regulars.'

In this series of battles, Jackson, in effect, did with the British army at Chalmette what the USS *Constitution* had done with the Royal Navy with the defeat of HMS *Guerriere*.

This time no one could consider what happened at Chalmette was a fluke. Jackson's decisive win washed away any derision for the young republic that had existed until then.

With this battle, many historians consider that the American Revolutionary War had been brought to a proper conclusion and the United States entered the stage of the world's great powers as an equal.

But this book, on a smaller scale, is about two combatants: a British Commodore and an American privateer Captain engaged in a struggle over that same sense of equality. It will be, as the larger war was, a bitter struggle.

Let us return to their story.

A Naval Incident at Horta

Paul Estronza La Violette

The Privateer Rambler *in the Pearl River, China. Built 1813, Medford, Mass., 318 tons. Oil, unsigned. (Courtesy Peabody Essex Museum)*

Chapter 3

LATE AFTERNOON, 26 SEPTEMBER

Captain Reid stood on the quarterdeck of the *General Armstrong,* watching the heavily laden barges provide the needed water to his ship.

Dabney's influence with the Azoreans was well demonstrated by the new supplies being brought aboard. With the requested water, a great deal of fresh fruit was handed up to the eager seamen. In addition, a line with netting attached was also lowered to bring aboard several crates of chickens and, after that, similar crates of small pigs and one with a rather noisy goat.

When the line to its crate slipped, one pig broke loose and the men made a great deal of noise chasing it around the deck. Reid, realizing things were going smoothly, turned and spoke to his first Lieutenant, Fredrick. A. Worth.

"Once all the stores are aboard and secured, let the starboard watch have liberty ashore till midnight. Emphasize to the men that liberty ends at midnight. No exceptions. Things are a little touchy here. I want to be able to leave at first light."

Reid knew the sight and smell of the nearby town with all its lures was tempting. He had a good crew and, just as important, a cheerful crew. Actions, such as unexpected liberty, despite his apprehensions about the port, would help maintain that cheerfulness.

Unlike the pressed seamen who made up much of the crews on British Royal Navy ships, the ninety men in *General Armstrong*'s crew were all volunteers. They were experienced sailors hand-picked from the more than two hundred highly qualified men who had come forward in New York when the call went out that the *General Armstrong* needed a new crew.

They formed a polyglot assembly. More than half were American, about a half dozen of these being blacks and a number of full-blooded Indians and half-breeds. The rest were made up of almost all of the seafaring nations of Europe: Sweden, Denmark, the Netherlands, France, and Italy.

A few even had suspicious accents reflecting their origins to be Cornwall, Lincoln, and Dundee, men who may well have deserted at one time or another from the British Royal Navy. Despite this and a heterogeneous diversity of clothing, there was one uniformity, all wore their hair clubbed and neatly tied in a ribbon or leather tie-tie.

About a dozen of the men were marines. These were headed by an officer who, while not as regimented in his discipline as a Royal Marine officer, did go through great pains to keep them up to par. In an ordinary encounter, these men would man the ship's foretop and maintop as sharpshooters.

What was more important was the crew knew that the success of the voyage, and thus the money they individually received from this cruise, depended on both their abilities as seamen and, as an integral part of this, on their skill in using these abilities under the guidance of their captain to capture British commercial vessels.

Reid was the second captain of the *General Armstrong*. According to several sources, he replaced her first captain, Guy R. Champlin, who had been injured in an earlier action that involved a British man-of-war disguised as a privateer.

Although only thirty-one years old (Reid had just turned 31 the previous month), he had more than twenty years experience at sea both as a seaman before the mast and as a ship's commander. And, most importantly, he had seen his share of action during those twenty years.

Reid was born in 1783, the son of a former British naval officer. His father, Lieutenant John Reid, had been taken prisoner during a night boat attack at New London. As a prisoner, he had been given his parole, i.e., his promise not to try to escape, and placed under the supervision of a Judge Chester of Norwalk, Connecticut.

This was fatal as far as his career as a British naval officer was concerned. He fell in love with the judge's daughter, Rebecca Chester. Being young and in love, John Reid resigned his commission to remain in the United States and to marry Rebecca. Samuel Chester Reid was the result of their union.

Deciding to follow in his father's footsteps, at the age of eleven, young Samuel Reid went to sea. He enlisted as a 'powder monkey,' a boy who brought powder to the ship's guns during an engagement.

This was not unusual. Children such as the young Reid were used by all the world's navies of the period. The *General Armstrong*'s crew included such children. Many, as they got older, provided a rich source of experienced crews and even officers. Samuel Chester Reid was to be among the latter.

Reid quickly saw action during the Quasi-War with France and, captured by a French privateer, was confined for six months at Basseterre, Guadeloupe. On his release, he worked his way up to acting midshipman on the USS *Baltimore* in Commander Thomas Truxton's West India squadron. Gaining more and more experience, he became master of the brig, *Merchant,* in 1803.

Now, Reid stood on the deck of the *General Armstrong* as her Captain. He had come a long way from a young powder monkey to waiting for the American Consul of the Azores to come aboard his vessel.

Mr. Dabney arrived promptly at five, bringing with him several members of the small consulate, including his twenty-one-year-old son, Charles B. Dabney. (The younger Dabney would succeed his father as the American Consul after his death and, in turn, his son would succeed him.)

Reid invited them to a light supper that had been set up with a certain amount of ceremony on makeshift, cloth-covered tables under an awning on the now sparkling clean afterdeck.

The conversation among the consulate entourage and vessel officers became general, the party comfortable, and all enjoyed the splendid view they had of the harbor. Dabney had developed a high regard for Reid, and their conversation was comfortable and friendly. He had, as promised, brought a case of his wine and the two shared a glass of it as they looked out over the bay.

It was not until just at early dusk when a cry from the *General Armstrong's* lookout changed the relaxed note of the gathering.

"British brig to the north northeast."

The *Carnation* had rounded the large northern cape of the bay.

As Reid and Dabney left their table and hurried to the railing, the brig was seen entering the bay in the evening light. They continued to watch the British warship as she slowly moved closer and closer.

After awhile both men became aware that the brig moved across the harbor in a way that made it obvious she was headed straight for the *General Armstrong*.

***

As there will be an hour or two before *Carnation* fully makes its threatening maneuvers on the *General Armstrong,* let us talk about the role of privateers in the wars of this period. Privateers were not official U.S. Navy vessels, but were actually vessels owned by individuals that carried letters of marque (*marque*, from Old French meaning "to seize").

In essence, such a commission allowed a citizen, or a cartel of citizens, to equip a private vessel, such as the *General Armstrong,* as a man-of-war and send her forth under an experienced captain to capture enemy shipping. Once captured, the merchant vessels and their cargoes were considered prizes owned by the privateer's patron(s) or cartel.

This was an extremely lucrative practice, and these types of documents were commonplace in the 18th and early 19th centuries. In fact, both Great Britain and France had vast numbers of privateers sailing under letters of marque signed by their respective governments.

In all, licensing armed ships to act as privateers was a practical way for nations at war to enlarge their navies' ability to wage war on their enemy's commerce at no cost to themselves.

An essential point to remember is that privateers were not prepared to engage an enemy warship of the same class. Since there was no monetary gain from such an encounter, most privateers used their inherent speed to run from such encounters.

Although little has been written about American privateers in the War of 1812, they were an extraordinary asset to the American naval effort and one that Great Britain recognized as a great danger to their nation's commerce. It was a danger Great Britain went through a great deal of effort to eliminate.

The *Thais* and *Calypso* were examples of this effort. The primary mission of these two ships was to chase and capture American privateers. Horta was their duty station, but their real efforts were to seek out and capture American privateers, and they spent long periods at sea doing this.

Documents and letters related to Commodore Lloyd's squadron of three ships indicate that the main purpose of his present command was also to search for and capture American privateers.

There were compelling reasons for the deployment of British warships for this purpose. A good example is the success of the American privateer, *Chasseur,* captained by Thomas Boyle. On his first voyage in 1814, Boyle sailed to the British Isles where he unmercifully harassed the region's British merchant fleet. During this one cruise, *Chasseur* is reported to have captured or sunk seventeen British vessels.

In an audacious act, he released a captured merchant vessel with a notice to the king. The notice was to be posted on the door of Lloyd's of London, the famous shipping underwriters. In it he declared the entire British Isles were under naval blockade by *Chasseur*!

Naturally, this sent the British shipping community into a panic and caused the Admiralty to call warships home from the American war to guard merchant convoys closer to Great Britain.

The *General Armstrong* was purposely made to raid commercial shipping. She was built specifically as a privateer in 1812 in a New York's East River shipyard. She had been designed by two brothers, Adam and Noah Brown, who, during the War of 1812, specialized in the construction of privateers.

No good picture is available of the *General Armstrong*, but it appears she was a little over 120 feet long, carried six 9-pound long guns, three to a side. In addition, she carried the immense 42-pounder long gun mentioned earlier on a swivel mount that allowed the gun to be turned to any angle and fired despite the vessel's heading.

Thus a broadside from the *General Armstrong* would launch sixty-nine pounds of iron at an enemy vessel, certainly not as much as a broadside from a British warship of equal size, but well enough to intimidate a merchant vessel into realizing her best interests were to surrender.

A Naval Incident at Horta

THE HISTORY OF *LONG TOM*

In 1798 the French line of battleship Hoche *was captured by a British squadron, and her main battery of 42-pound long guns was purchased and shipped to New York to be part of the city's harbor defense. However, one gun was rejected, and that gun was retained by the original supplier.*

In 1804 the supplier entered into a contract with the Emperor of Haiti, whose country was at war with France. Three vessels were fitted out; one was the Samson, *with the rejected 42- pounder mounted amidships on a pivot platform.*

In its first action, the gun carried away the foremast of a large French privateer pursing the three vessels. When the Haiti contract was completed in 1807, the original supplier purchased Samson *for merchant service and had the gun dismounted. It lay in a New York City shipyard until, with the start of the War of 1812, New York became alive with fitting out privateers, one of these being the* General Armstrong. *The gun was purchased for two hundred and fifty dollars and mounted on a pivot on the* General Armstrong,

Unquestionably, the 42-pounder long gun would go a long way to increase that intimidation. Because of the size of this gun, *General Armstrong* could engage an enemy vessel from more than a mile away, farther than any gun in the *Armstrong's* main battery of 9-pounders. Once fired, the 42-pound ball could set up a huge splash. Witnessing this, a fleeing merchant vessel would do well to think twice about continuing to run.

More importantly for the story of the battle that was about to unfold, the 42-pound ball fired by the gun could hull (i.e., penetrate the hull) of the British brig *Carnation* while the *Carnation* was still too far away to effectively use her main battery of carronades.

***

Let us return to the early evening gathering aboard the *General Armstrong*.

Reid lowered the glass with which he had watched the approaching British warship and turned to his guest.

"Is that, sir, *Thais* or *Calypso?*"

Dabney, grasping the railing, stared for a long moment at the oncoming warship.

"Neither!" he said finally, "I have no idea who she is."

He turned from the advancing brig to face Reid.

"Horta is a neutral port, Captain Reid. Whatever that vessel's intent, I cannot believe the British will have the audacity to start any type of action right here in the port. Please, sir. Look around us. Anything they do will take place in full view of the entire town!"

Reid nodded. "Whoever she is, I'm afraid I don't have the luxury of giving her the benefit of a doubt. I regret this abrupt ending to what has been a pleasant visit, but I must, as captain of this vessel, begin preparations for any possibilities. I must ask you and your guests to leave immediately for your own safety."

He motioned to his coxswain, who had been standing by at the rail.

"I will have our boat take you and your people ashore and rig the vessel for the worst. I assure you we will not initiate anything. But my duty as the master of this vessel is to do everything I can to defend her. I sincerely hope that these precautions will eventually prove to be unnecessary, and we will be able to meet again tomorrow under less strenuous conditions."

"I hope so, sir. I will speak to the British Vice Consul, Mr. Parkin, when we go ashore. I saw him earlier in town. Perhaps he can tell me what is going on."

With this, Dabney bowed and headed to the opening in the side rail where the other members of the consul's group already waited to depart.

Captain Reid watched them leave and then turned his attention to the oncoming brig that had been identified by one of the crew as HMS *Carnation*. As he raised his glass to study the inverted image of the vessel in its lens, he heard a cry from the lookout.

"Deck there, I see two more British ships rounding the northern point. Looks like a 74 and a frigate."

It was *Plantagenet* and *Rota*.

This erased Reid's hesitancy. He turned to his first lieutenant.

"Mr. Worth, have all hands go to their stations immediately and clear the deck for battle. Have them don their leather helmets, and have them be extremely quiet and stay low. Tell the men I particularly insist on their remaining so. I do not wish the British to see our preparations and use them as an excuse to start an unprovoked action.

"See that all the guns are loaded. Traverse 'Long Tom' to an angle in the general direction of that brig. If we must shoot, we might as well start off with our heaviest means of arguing."

It was not without reason that *General Armstrong* had a huge crew. In addition to needing a large body of fighting men when boarding an enemy vessel, it took a large number of men to man her several guns. Each 9-pounder took eight men to arm and fire. Since normally only one side would be firing, that meant a one-sided broadside by the 9-pounders required twenty-four men; firing both sides required twice that.

The 42-pounder, Long Tom, took ten men and even this was barely enough, as the swivel mounting had proven to be shaky. In the last series of practice firing, the men's footing had been unsteady, especially when hauling the gun back to the gun port after firing. Reid had not had time to repair the mount, and it would give him trouble in the coming actions.

There were other crewmen needed besides those actually engaged in firing the guns. There were the vessel's doctor and his assistants, the powder monkeys and the like to supply ammunition and powder, the men needed to sail the vessel, and the men standing by as repair crews should the vessel be damaged and, of course, there were men for the inevitable boarding.

In addition, any successful cruise as a privateer required prize crews. These would be needed to man whatever vessel was captured and take it back to a friendly or neutral port. The more ships taken, the more prize crews were needed. There were no special crews for this; the men were taken from the general crew and usually one of the vessel's officers.

All of this called for a crowded vessel and cramped quarters. Now, as the *Carnation* came on and action threatened, the need for this number of men was not one that Reid begrudged.

There was an added almost comic twist to the *General Armstrong* crew's preparations for battle.

On the morning after they had sailed out from Sandy Hook, Reid had issued each man a leather helmet with a metal brace that reached below the neck.

Such protection, while unusual, was not unknown in vessel engagements of the time. In fact, other naval vessels had begun using some type of head protection. The dropping of spars, pulleys, and gear was one of the chief causes of injuries during an action.

As Reid explained when he handed out the leather helmets, the helmets provided each man a double protection. The obvious one was for falling gear and to deflect wooden splinters from the enemy's balls smashing parts of the wooden ship. The other was a defense against cutlasses when boarding an enemy vessel. Hand guns could only be fired once in the swarming melee that such boarding consisted of, and it was during these times that the enemy's cutlasses posed the real danger.

"Besides," Reid is reported to have told the men as, with a tremendous amount of laughter, they first tried on the helmets, "you look like a bunch of mean devils. If that takes a man aback when you are having a go at him, you will have that many seconds to do him than you would have had otherwise."

The men had looked at each other, and the laughter grew anew, even louder than before. Reid was right; their appearance individually was startling and, as a group, they did indeed look fearsome. Reid then opened a large chest and produced another piece of personal armament to give to each of the men, a broad cutlass for boarding.

"With that sharp rascal in your hand and your ugly leather helmet on your head, anyone who sees you boarding their ship, will think twice before giving you an argument."

Now these same men were huddled below the ship's railing, their helmets on and their cutlasses stored near at hand. To Reid, they looked as fearsome a group of men as he had promised they would be.

Satisfied by what he saw, he renewed his watch of the British warship. He realized they would need that bit of psychological help if the men in the oncoming *Carnation* attempted to board.

Reid, on the other hand, chose to expose his person in a complete reversal of the crew. He remained standing highly visible on the quarterdeck, wearing the same plain white shirt, less the dress coat, in which he had greeted the American consul and his party.

Reid felt if there was an encounter, what he looked like would be important. He thought it essential that his appearance gave no excuse to the British that the Americans were ready and wanted an excuse to fight.

Meanwhile, *Carnation*, after a great deal of signaling with the other two warships, was a great deal closer. Although she had slowed for a considerable time for an exchange of signals, she had not veered from her initial heading since her first appearance. There was now no doubt of her course; she was headed directly toward the *General Armstrong*.

Lt. Worth joined Reid in watching the *Carnation's* approach.

"Jonathon says that's the *Carnation* and the frigate standing in with the 74 is the *Rota*. He seen both ships in Boston awhile back just before the war. He don't know who the 74 is, not that it really matters."

"You're right. Whatever ship it is, she's big enough to mean trouble."

Reid continued to watch the frigate with his glass. So this was *Rota*. She looked formidable, much more menacing than the brig. He wondered if the officers had been rehearsing a play to present in Horta tonight. With this in mind, he lowered his glass and looked over at his first lieutenant.

"I'm sorry to say this, Mr. Worth, but you will have to cancel liberty ashore tonight. Please tell the men."

Worth smiled, shook his head. "I'm sure they will understand, Captain."

Carnation anchored a short distance from the *General Armstrong*. A constant exchange of signals had been maintained with the other two warships. This exchange now intensified, lasting some time.

Then the exchange stopped, and *Carnation* began lowering all four of her large launches into the water and passing weapons down to them. All of this was done quite openly. What was more menacing was the orders that were being given carried far over the bay's calm waters and, although distorted, could be heard on the *Armstrong.*

What little they could understand erased any doubt of the aggressive nature of *Carnation's* intentions. Reid, hearing and watching, felt he had no choice on what course he should take.

He turned to his first. "I think this is becoming to be a little too close, Mr. Worth. Have the men man the sweeps and, when ready, put a buoy on the cable and cut it loose. Have them do this as quickly as they can and still be quiet about it. Turn us about and bring us closer to shore, if you will."

He raised his glass so as to see the parapet of the fort. There was no one there.

"Let's move ourselves just under the guns of the old fort. I don't think the Portuguese will defend their neutrality and use their guns to protect us, but it may well cause those people in the boats to think twice at whatever it is they want to do."

In a few moments the *General Armstrong's* sweeps were extended from her sides and the crew, their helmets momentarily removed, started rowing these long oars, moving the vessel toward the old fort looming beyond them in the night.

Seeing the *General Armstrong* slip its anchor and begin to move away, *Carnation* slipped her anchor as well and, dropping her topsails, hastily made sail to the southern part of the harbor. Reid shook his head in exasperation. It was a blatant move to prevent the privateer from trying to leave the port.

The four heavily armed and manned launches, now free of the vessel, proceeded toward the *General Armstrong*, rowing at a high rate of speed through the dying light.

***

Meanwhile, Consul Dabney had begun a night-long series of diplomatic efforts to ease what was about to become an armed conflict.

He sent his son, Charles, to the Portuguese Governor's residence to inform him of what was unfolding and to ask him to do whatever was in his power as representative of the Portuguese king to stop it from escalating.

Dabney also sent an inquiry to the British Vice Consul, asking him if he was aware of what was happening and if he could do anything to help. There is no record of his receiving a reply from Mr. Parkin.

As an observer later wrote of what took place that night: "It being about full of moon, the night perfectly clear and calm, we could see every movement that was made."

As the night progressed, there would be much to see.

A Naval Incident at Horta

Paul Estronza La Violette

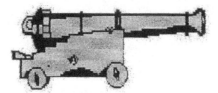 

A Naval Incident at Horta

Chapter 4

THE FIRST ACTION, EARLY EVENING, 26 SEPTEMBER

It was a dramatic setting.

At nearly eight o'clock, the early evening light from the setting sun, so bright earlier, had dimmed. The nearly full moon, rising to one side of the bay, was now the main light shining on the water. However, in the many reports of witnesses to the scene, the moon was so bright it illuminated the arena of battle as if all that occurred took place in broad daylight.

There was little wind; indeed, there would be little wind throughout the night. The surface of the bay was perfectly calm except for the white splash of the oars of the four launches, each carrying between twenty and thirty well-armed men, pulling swiftly toward the privateer.

Reid watched the armed launches, gauging their speed. They moved faster than he had anticipated earlier, and he was worried. After a few moments, he realized the *General*

Armstrong would not make it to the cover of the old fort before the launches overtook her.

He called out to his first lieutenant. "Mr. Worth, cease with the sweeps. Have the men bring them in as quickly as possible. Then let go the port anchor, and set springs on the cable so as to bring us broadside to those boats.

"Again, try to do this without exposing the readiness of the crew any more than you need."

Lt. Worth quickly had the long oars shipped and, with several men, stooping low, scrambled to the bow, where they let go the port anchor. Working quickly, they applied a heavy line to the anchor chain, and, with that line following them in the water alongside the ship, ran aft. Once there, they dragged the dripping line out of the water and began to pull it taut.

Slowly, with one end of the line secured to the bow anchor and the other end being pulled at the stern, the vessel began to swing until it became broadside to the approaching British launches. This done the men secured the line and, still maintaining a low profile, scurried back to their battle stations and, re-donning their battle helmets, dropped to sitting positions below the railing to wait.

At this point the American and British accounts begin to differ sharply and a brief explanation is warranted as to which version will be followed and why.

I have provided both Captain Reid and Post-Captain Lloyd's final reports of the actions as appendices to this book. I also added, as a third appendix, an account of the battle as seen from the shore by a knowledgeable British observer.

Finally, I have included, later in this book, a letter from the governor of Fayal, who witnessed what happened and, in the letter, the governor agrees with the American account rather than Lloyd's version of what took place.

There are other accounts of the actions, e.g., those of the American Consul, John Dabney, and, years later, his son. Both tend to agree with Reid's account of what happened, but these accounts are obviously biased to support the American rendition.

Finally, there is no question but that Lloyd attempted a *coup de main* with the heavily armed and manned boat action. In fact, in a letter, the British Admiralty Board's First Secretary, John W. Croker, saw it for what it was and criticized Lloyd for making such a blatant attempt.

Based on the available writings, I will stay with Reid's description of what actually took place, although I will interject a British account at the end of this chapter for completeness.

One British launch, considerably in advance of the other three, approached *General Armstrong's* stern. Reid, his speaking trumpet in hand and still in his shirtsleeves, walked to the after rail and hailed the approaching boat, telling the officer in charge that his was an American vessel and that the launch was to stay clear or he would open fire.

Reid later states he warned the launch four times, but no answer was returned. The launch continued its approach until it was alongside *General Armstrong's* stern.

The British officer (*Plantagenet's* second Lieutenant, Thomas Faussett) then gave the order to "toss oars" and, using their boat hooks, the British seamen and marines hauled the launch under the port quarter of the privateer. The officer is then said to have cried out, "Fire and board, my lads."

As the men rose from their seats, Reid felt he could wait no longer and gave the order to fire into the boat.

The British were prepared to return fire and there resulted an almost simultaneous explosion of small guns from both the crew of the *General Armstrong* and the men in the launch.

Men were hurt on both sides.

On the *General Armstrong,* one of the American crew was instantly killed by the British fire and Reid's first lieutenant fell seriously wounded. But it was in the launch that there were the most casualties with many of its occupants severely wounded.

Using the same boathooks they had used to draw them to the *General Armstrong's* stern, the British seamen began to push the boat away while simultaneously crying out for quarter, i.e., for mercy and for the Americans to cease firing.

During this encounter at the stern, the other three boats pulled up on *General Armstrong's* port side and, hearing the action at the stern, opened fire on those of the *General Armstrong* crew whom they could discern behind the railing.

This was instantly answered by the privateer crew, who let go with massed small arms fire. This was augmented by a rain of grape from the several swivel guns Reid had mounted on the railing.

The effect on the men in these three launches was worse than that which had occurred in the British boat at the stern. In moments the air was filled with the groans of wounded and dying men.

Now, in near sinking condition and with obvious heavy losses, the boats pulled away from the *General Armstrong*. As with the stern British launch, these men also cried out for quarter. On hearing this, Captain Reid ordered a cease fire and allowed the damaged launches, with their injured, to retreat back to *Carnation*.

Satisfied that the fighting, at least temporarily, was over, Reid made sure his first lieutenant was taken below to the care of the surgeon and his aides. This done, he asked for a quick tally to show that no other member of his crew had been injured in the attack. This tally showed they had escaped the battle with amazingly few serious casualties (there were just the two). There were minor injuries, but none that would cause any of the crew to not be ready for another action.

Reid then ordered the crew to weigh anchor and, pulling out the ship's sweeps once more, had the vessel rowed toward the shore and the dark structure of the Portuguese fort. When they were about twenty yards from the walls of the fort, he ordered the sweeps pulled in and, in the shallow water, moored the vessel parallel to the shore, starboard side out.

The vessel was now in the shadow formed by the old fort and the rising full moon Looking up at the stone walls looming dark and silent above them, Reid realized he would receive no help from the ancient Portuguese fort or its garrison, if such a garrison, indeed, existed. In fact, there had been no evidence of Portuguese defensive support since the action started.

The Portuguese might have declared the Port of Horta to be neutral, but for the British to have made such a blatant attack, spoke little of the Portuguese ability to defend that neutrality. Anchored in the silent shadow of the fort, Reid realized that Portuguese military assistance was not to be had. If there was to be any armed defense of the privateer, it would have to be from the *General Armstrong's* crew. It was not an enviable prospect. Being near the fort was, in essence, being up against the wall.

The Fort of Santa Cruz was originally built for protection against Moorish pirates in the 16th century. It was a star fort with large pointed star-like projections in its outer walls. Reid had anchored the *General Armstrong* close to the walls on the north side of the seaward facing star. The landing mole he had used earlier in the day was on the south side.

Reid was probably right about expecting no aid from the fort or its garrison. In 1775 Captain Cook called at Horta for a short visit. After inspecting Forte de Santa Cruz, he wrote:

> On landing we realized why the Portuguese had not returned our salute - their gun carriages were rotten and they were afraid to fire their guns ... the garrison was supposed to be 100 men but they had only 40, undisciplined and without proper arms.

An old print of Horta and Forte de Santa Cruz. It is believed the General Armstrong *was anchored just to the right of the center embattlement of the fort. The mole used for landing was located to the left of the fort.*

However, Forte de Santa Cruz was to be given some later attention and dressing up that relied heavily on this night and the next day's actions.

In 1821, a Portuguese inspector reported the fort to be in good repair. It should have been, for the armament found in the fort in 1821, and somewhat still found today, included the six 9-pounders and the 42-pound "Long Tom" that had once belonged to the vessel now anchored in the shadow of its walls, the American privateer, *General Armstrong*.

But 1821 was several years in the future. Let us return to about ten o'clock on the night of 26 September 1814, when Captain Reid looked on a grim night scene and faced the reality of his predicament.

The moon was still out, although slightly higher in the sky than before the British assault. The vessel still lay sequestered in the fort's shadow. The air was surprisingly still; there was almost no wind. In front of him, the water, lit by the moon despite the hard set of the mid-Atlantic tidal current, was just as calm as it was before the action, less than an hour earlier.

But now men were dead.

As Reid looked over the chilling remnants of the recent action, he knew only too well that more was to come, much more. The British would not let what happened go unanswered. Cards had been laid on the table that must be played by the players. Whether he liked it or not, Reid was one of the two players.

Reid made his way forward and, calling his remaining officers around him, began making preparations for the eventual second hand.

***

It is interesting to note that the account given by the British naval historian, Admiral William James, as to what happened that early evening in September 1814, is quite different from the American account written by Captain Reid:

> Captain Lloyd sent Lieutenant Robert Faussett, in the *Plantagenet's* pinnace, into the port, to ascertain the force of the schooner and to what nation she belonged.
>
> Owing to the strength of the tide, and to the circumstance of the schooner getting under way and dropping fast astern, the boat drifted nearer to her than had been intended.
>
> The American privateer hailed, and desired the boat to keep off, but that was impracticable owing to the quantity of stern-way on the schooner. The *General Armstrong* then opened her fire, and, before the boat could get out of gun-shot, killed two and wounded seven of her men.

(Admiral William James, *Naval History of Great Britain* - Vol. VI)

A Naval Incident at Horta

Not everyone was in agreement with Admiral James' account of the Horta action as reported by Lloyd.

In Chapter 9, a letter from the British Admiralty Board addressed to Commodore Lloyd will be presented. In the letter, the Admiralty Board, especially the First Secretary, states emphatically to Lloyd what they think of his actions and the excuses he sent them for doing what he did.

It is not a nice letter.

Paul Estronza La Violette

*A British boat attack in the Battle of Lake Borgne, War of 1812
watercolor, 1840, artist unknown
(Courtesy The Mariners' Museum, Newport News Naval Archives)*

A Naval Incident at Horta

Chapter 5

NINE PM THROUGH MIDNIGHT, 26 SEPTEMBER

Captain Reid stood on the quarterdeck of the *General Armstrong* and watched through his glass the scurrying boat movements taking place among the British warships farther out in the bay.

The *Carnation*, after quickly recovering its four heavily damaged boats with their dead and wounded, had sailed to join the other vessels of the squadron. Once there, boats could be seen going back and forth between the ships, with *Plantagenet* their main focus.

As Reid watched, it became evident a council of war was taking place aboard the flagship. That a more formidable attack on the *General Armstrong* would soon occur was, in his mind, a foregone conclusion. His biggest problem was he did not know what would be the nature of such an attack.

There were several attack venues open to the British.

Given the British commodore's seeming indifference to the Portuguese neutrality, there existed an outside chance the British might land a force of marines farther north in the harbor.

Tactically this could be a strong move. Once landed, they could march through the town and attack the vessel from the shore, using the fort behind Reid as their fire base. Even muskets from the height of the walls could rain havoc on *General Armstrong's* crew.

But Reid realized such an attack would be too flagrant a violation of the port's neutrality; besides, any such force, wherever it landed in the harbor, would be visible from his vessel, and he would have ample time to rig a strong defense, even preempting the British action by having his men take control of the fort walls.

No, he was sure any new assault would come via the broad stretch of water in front of him. But what type of assault?

Carnation, with its shallow draft in comparison to the other ships of the squadron, could move in close and attack using the immense superiority of her eighteen guns. Fired in broadsides of nine to a side, these large poundage "smashers" would wreck havoc on the crew and could easily hull the vessel with just a few broadsides. And, it is doubtful *Carnation* would stop with just a few broadsides.

To defend against this, Reid would have to engage *Carnation* while she was beyond the effective range of her carronades, yet within range of his 42- and 9-pound long guns. Given the longer range his guns had over *Carnation's*, there was a chance they might disable the brig so she would have to retire before getting close enough to open up with her devastating broadsides.

Although slim, this would be his main hope.

The problem was that by concentrating their fire on the *Carnation,* the Americans would leave their vessel essentially undefended against a simultaneous smaller, but deadly, attack by British boats.

As he continued his reasoning, it became plain that a combined attack by *Carnation* and a large number of armed launches would be the logical strategy for a second British assault. It was this combination for which he had to prepare his defense.

Accepting this inevitability, he turned to his two remaining officers and began his preparations.

The first of these efforts was to double the fire power on *General Armstrong's* starboard side. Reid ordered the three 9-pound port-side guns be brought over to the starboard side and new gun ports cut to accommodate them. This arrangement gave him six 9-pound long cannon facing his attackers; on any vessel this would be a respectable and deadly battery of guns.

Firing these six guns presented a new problem on how best to fire them. In the coming action, broadsides would give Reid no advantage. A better strategy would be to fire each gun as fast as its gun crew could fire, rather than limit the firing of all the guns to the timing of the slowest gun crew.

In addition, the independent firing of the 9-pounders would psychologically work better to the privateer's advantage than if they fired broadsides. In effect, the British in the attacking launches would be faced with almost non-stop blasts of cannon fire.

Reid also worried that the firing of his guns would put tremendous pressure on the anchor, possibly dislodging it from its hold on the bottom. Although his plan to independently fire the guns would help spread the pressure on the anchor, the possibility of it being dislodged by the pounding of the almost continuous gun recoils was something he could not ignore.

To mitigate this, Reid decided to put two anchors out and ordered this to be done. The second anchor had to be brought up from its place in the ship's hold, since the starboard anchor was still attached to a buoy farther out in the bay. After a great deal of work in the half-light that the battle lanterns made available, this was done and the second anchor was set firmly in the bottom.

Then, after vigorously testing their holds, springs were put on both anchor cables to maintain equal pressure and the new arrangement tested.

There were several advantages to the new anchorage. The bracing furnished by the anchors and the lack of vessel movement meant that the gun crews had a steady platform, not as stable as if they were actually ashore, but a good substitute. Aiming the guns from such a platform would increase the accuracy of the guns when they fired. Accuracy would be the one factor most needed if the *Carnation* elected to come.

Another advantage of being anchored was there would not be a need for any of the crew to handle the sails or to con the vessel. Essentially, all ninety men in the *Armstrong's* crew would be available to man and fire the long cannons or swivel guns or, in the event they were boarded by the attackers, they would defend the vessel with cutlasses and small arms.

Reid had netting stretched completely around the privateer to make it difficult for the attackers to board and had pikes strategically laid out along the railing to allow the men to jab at the enemy between the netting as they tried to board.

In addition to *Carnation's* guns, Reid knew the attacking launches would also carry large carronades. He had the men's hammocks brought up from below and tied to the starboard railing and around the ship's masts. These would act as cushions to catch grapeshot from the British launch's carronades, as well as reduce casualties due to splinters.

Small chain was wrapped about the spars as reinforcement to their bindings. This would insure that if cordage was cut, the heavy spars and blocks would not fall and maim the defenders below. To further defend against spars and whatever blocks, cordage, and debris that might fall, Reid had splinter netting rigged head high over the entire vessel.

To add to the privateer's small arms firepower, he had more swivel guns brought up and placed along the ship's railing, each fully loaded with grape. He also had loaded blunderbusses and pistols placed strategically around the deck.

A British naval blunderbuss (Courtesy of Morristown National Historical Park)

When these preparations had been completed, Reid called the crew together and told them how he wanted them to defend the vessel in the coming action. He was determined that no matter what the outcome, the men of the *General Armstrong* would give a good account of themselves.

At the start of his talk, he emphasized the closeness of the odds they had in succeeding in the coming action and emphasized that the timing and the rapidity of their gunfire would be the factors that would give them the edge they would need to succeed.

The firing plan Reid dictated was a little involved due to the fact that they did not know if the British would make a combined brig/armed-launch attack. The type ammunition used by the guns for one type attack was decidedly different from the other.

At the beginning of the action, at the moment the British came within range, the guns would fire. This would be the start of a tightly choreographed firing.

If they elected to fire at the *Carnation*, ball-and-chain shot would be used exclusively by all of the *Armstrong* guns. If it was a combined attack of *Carnation* and armed launches, the *Armstrong's* Long Tom would concentrate on trying to hull

Carnation, while the six 9-pounders would concentrate their fire on the launches.

The 42-pounder, Long Tom, because of its longer range, would fire first. Then, as the enemy got closer, the six 9-pounders would open up, with each 9-pounder firing independently of the others.

Just before the launches got close enough for boarding, the guns would fire a triple load of grape and then the gun crews were to secure and seal each gun's port. Reid laid great emphasis on this last. He did not want any of the enemy boarders to use an open gun port to gain access to the privateer's deck. After securing the gun ports, the rest of the defense would rely on the men wielding pikes, blunderbusses, pistols and, finally, cutlasses.

Reid stationed the marines in the ship's fighting tops in the fore- and main-masts. From these high positions and armed with blunderbusses, as well as muskets and pistols, these men could fire down on the launch crews as they tried to board. Unlike the men on deck, who would be busy using pikes and cutlasses, the marines would have a chance to reload their weapons and, hopefully, reuse them to reduce the number of boarders.

Blunderbusses were nice in this regard, as with their wide mouths they were easy to reload, especially in the heat of battle when a steady hand was not always part of a combatant's equipment. And the spread of their shot was a deadly force, especially when fired downward

In essence, as Reid talked, it became evident that it would be the men's fighting ability as individuals that would decide the outcome.

As they prepared for the night's action, he realized he no longer had the valued services of his first lieutenant. Worth was in the dispensary, seriously wounded. His advice and services in the coming action would be missed.

He delegated his second lieutenant, Mr. Alex Williams, to take charge of the forward division, and his third lieutenant, Mr. Robert Johnson, the men in the ship's waist. As he wanted to take personal command of the Long Tom, Reid would stay aft to command the after guard.

Satisfied he had done all he could reasonably do about setting up an adequate defense, he joined the after division with its 42-pounder, Long Tom. The men there had already loaded the gun with round shot and sat waiting about the stern, looking across the water at the British ships.

About twenty yards from the moored privateer, the dark walls of the old Portuguese fort loomed, a massive, yet unfortunately impotent, spectator of their plight.

Following the first action, a number of spectators expecting that there would be a second part to the night's actions had come to the fort. Some of these were visible at the parapets.

Reid, seeing this, was troubled.

He had not counted on spectators being so close. They seemed to be in a dangerous position to him, and he weighed the advisability of sending some men up to ask them to leave due to the danger of errant gunfire.

After some consideration, he decided not to; he really had no authority to chase any of the local population from their own fort. On the plus side, he felt a violent disturbance among these same spectators would warn him if the British tried to somehow use the fort for a rear attack.

Reid, having examined the huge gun and the crew's preparations, looked forward at the 9-pounders and their crews. There, the men sat waiting; many even dozed at their positions. He nodded to himself. The men knew an attack was coming and none had left his battle station since the earlier action; they deserved a little sleep.

Satisfied he had done everything he could do, he leaned back against the large gun's carriage and began a long wait; maybe, if he was lucky, a little sleep as well.

As it turned out it would be a long wait, but no sleep.

***

News of the upcoming battle had spread through the small port town, as well as the surrounding countryside of Fayal. Large fires, scattered around the broad cusp of hills surrounding the moonlit bay, were visible as spectators gathered there for a grander view.

People also came into Horta in horse-drawn wagons to see the spectacle of a night naval battle up close. The windows of the houses nearest the scene were filled with spectators, and the sea wall was crowded with people wanting to view the night action first hand.

As stated earlier, the ramparts of the old Portuguese fort also had their collection of spectators. These included John Dabney and his son, Charles. Both Dabneys would later write first-hand accounts of what was about to happen.

Consul Dabney had been busy doing his diplomatic best to quash the escalating situation. Earlier, he had sent Charles with a strong note to Portuguese Governor Elias Jose Ribeiro. In it he demanded, in the strongest language possible as a representative of the American Government, that the governor provide some type of official protection for the *General Armstrong* and her crew in their role as neutral guests of the Portuguese government.

FAYAL, 26th September 1814, 9 o'clock P.M.

TO HIS EXCELLENCY THE GOVERNOR OF FAYAL:

> Sir, — In violation of the neutrality, that His Royal Highness, the Prince Regent of Portugal has pledged himself to cause to be observed in his dominions in the present war between the United States and England, the British Ships of war now in the harbor have just sent four or five armed boats to surprise and carry off the American Privateer

"General Armstrong."

    Captain Reid, then and now at anchor under the guns of the Castle, where he conceived himself perfectly protected and secure. The boats were repulsed, but a second and more formidable attack is premeditated; I therefore require Your Excy. to protect this American vessel, either by force, or by such representations to the British Commander, as will cause him to desist from any further violence. I also request your Excy. to give leave for the American seamen now here, to go on board the said American brig to assist in defending her, if the English should attack her a second time.

JOHN B. DABNEY

    The Portuguese governor really had no concrete way to force the British to stop their actions as Dabney's note demanded. All the governor could diplomatically do was to dispatch a similar strong note to Commodore Lloyd, requesting him to respect the neutrality of the port and to immediately abstain from further hostilities against the *General Armstrong.*

    In his note, Dabney also asked the governor to allow thirty-two American seamen, stranded in Fayal, to go on board the *General Armstrong* to help in the privateer's defense. These merchant seamen had been captured when British warships seized their ships as part of the earlier blockade of unauthorized shipments to France. They had been housed in a nearby abandoned convent at Dabney's expense and were understandably eager to help in the defense of the *General Armstrong.*

    The governor felt, quite rightly, that sending more Americans to help defend the besieged vessel would only enflame an already escalating situation. He sent a note back to Dabney denying the request.

We shall shortly hear more concerning these stranded mariners.

FAYAL, September 26th, 1814, 10 o'clock P. M.

TO THE COMMANDER OF THE BRITISH NAVAL FORCE IN THIS PORT:

Sir, — In this port under the dominion of his Royal Highness the Prince Regent of Portugal, lies at anchor the United States brig of war "General Armstrong", which has been obliged to come here from want of water. The neutrality of Portugal acknowledged by his Britannic Majesty, requires that the commanders of his naval forces should respect the vessels here.

The Governor has therefore the honour to request at your hands, that you will abstain from any hostility against the said vessel; and he avails himself of this occasion to give to the Commander in chief the consideration which he merits. His obedient servant

ELIAS JOSE RIBERIRO

Commodore Lloyd's rather pompous and strongly worded reply was later handed to Lt. Matterface to give to the governor's envoy.

HIS BRITANNIC MAJESTY'S SHIP PLANTAGENET, Sept. 26th 1814.

Sir, — Permit me to inform you that one of the boats of his Britannic Majesty's ship under my command was, without the slightest provocation fired on by the American schooner "General Armstrong," in consequence of which two men were killed and seven were wounded; and that the neutrality of the port, which I had determined to respect, has been thereby violated.

In consequence of this outrage, I am determined to take possession of the vessel, and I hope that you will order your fort to protect the force employed for that purpose. With due respect I remain sir, your obedient servant,

THE COMMANDER OF HIS BRITANNIC MAJESTY'S FORCES

The last two letters were exchanged just prior to the second night attack.

At about 9 P.M., as the *General Armstrong's* crew waited at their gun stations, the *Carnation* was observed standing in with some twelve boats in tow. When just out of range of the *General Armstrong* long guns, the launches cast off from *Carnation* and took station in three divisions in the cover of a large shoal of rocks.

The *Carnation*, after releasing its tow, kept under way. She appeared, by her actions, to be positioning herself as a backup for the boats in case the privateer tried to escape.

As they waited, it was not clear to Reid and his men why the British were loitering behind the rocks. They saw them move about in a seemingly meaningless fashion as the *Carnation* assumed a position just to the south, but nothing else happened.

Time stretched on for an hour and then some, but finally, at midnight, the launches began a definite movement to move clear of the rocks. They formed a long line as they did so and, rowing vigorously, commenced their attack. The second assault on the *General Armstrong* had begun.

Diplomacy had failed and the men of the *General Armstrong* were on their own.

Paul Estronza La Violette

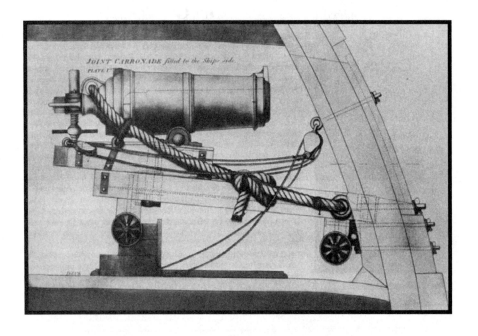

An old print of a naval carronade mounted on the gun deck of an 1812 man of war. Note the gun's carriage mounting. Warships could remount these cannon in their boats - cutters, pinnaces, launches, barges, etc. - to give them firepower for the boat actions such as used by the British in their night attack against the General Armstrong *in the Bay of Horta.*

A FEW NOTES ON GUNS

You will have already noticed that long cannons (sometimes referred to as "long guns") and carronades are the principal guns the two protagonists used. As these two types of guns play a major role in the actions that follow, let us talk about the two guns, their differing advantages and the type ammunition they use.

There were good reasons for each side's use of the two type guns. They were completely different weapons, each with their own advantages and disadvantages.

Carronades were the guns being carried by more and more British warships of the period since they fit with the strategy of getting as close to the enemy as possible and hammering away until the enemy was beaten into submission. Conversely, the long cannon were the guns American warships normally used, although they too were using carronades more and more.

This was not a hard and fast rule. Both sides tended to mix the two weapons, and more and more carronades were being carried on American warships. A view of the armament aboard the preserved *Constitution* today shows a vessel armed with a mix of each: thirty 24-pound long cannon and twenty 32-pound carronades (as well as two 24-pound long cannon as bow chasers).

To begin, carronades, rather than long cannon, are ideal guns to use on the attacking British launches or boats. They are shorter, lighter, require a smaller gun crew, and use less powder than their equivalent poundage long cannon.

Lighter, in this case, is a relative term. The carronades, while definitely lighter in weight than their equivalent long cannon, were nevertheless, as shown in the table on the opposite page, extremely heavy.

When long cannon are fired, the whole unit, gun and carriage, are hurled back by the recoil. Most injuries suffered by gun crews were the result of this recoil. On ships of the early 1800's, gun carriages were secured to the ship by a number of lines and pulleys. These transferred some of the shock of the recoil of these heavy guns to the ship's frame.

It was this sharp jolt of the guns' firing, transferred to the vessel, which was the cause of Reid's worry when he anchored the *General Armstrong* near the fort. He was afraid the shock of the large number of guns going off again and again from only one side of the vessel would dislodge one or both of the ship's anchors. As a result, he wisely decided they would fire the guns independently of one another, rather than together as a broadside.

Carronades have comparatively smaller recoil because of their reduced use of powder and the smaller gun mass. Thus, lighter gun carriages can be used. A carronade, when fired, slides in a special slot in its carriage and the lines securing the gun to the carriage, rather than the vessel, absorb the recoil.

For this reason carronades could be placed on large boats or launches, whereas the much heavier long cannon could not. When a carronade was fired aboard a boat, the special carriage absorbed the shock of the gun's firing and, as a result, did little to interfere with the boat's passage through the water.

The rate of fire between the carronade and its equivalent long cannon was also different. The 9-pound long cannon on the *General Armstrong* took about two minutes to reload and fire, the 42-pounder a little longer, slightly less than three minutes. Conversely, the carronades on the British launches could reload and fire at a rate of much less than two minutes.

However, given the crowded conditions on the launches, coupled with the launches inherent jerky movements, the firing rate was highly variable and even less accurate.

There were several serious trade offs for the carronade's advantages. Carronades did not have the range or the accuracy of long cannon; nor did they have quite the punch when hitting their target.

Part of this was due to the difference in the lengths of the two gun's barrels and part to the amount of gunpowder each used. Long cannon, such as the 9-pounders fired by the *General Armstrong*, used almost four times the amount of powder as the equivalent carronade 9-pounder.

It was the extra, very strong push, furnished by the long cannon's increased amount of powder, which hurled the shot farther than the same weight ball fired by a carronade.

Most importantly, when the long cannon ball hit what it was aimed at, say the hull of an enemy ship, it did so with tremendous inertial energy and the result was the hull was often hit hard enough to be punctured, or in the nautical parlance, 'hulled.'

Long Cannon / Carronade Comparison
12 - Pounder Equivalent Guns*

Gun	Gun Length	Shot Dia.	Weight of gun	Powder Charge	Range in yds.
Long Cannon	8'6"	4.4"	3,808 lbs.	4 lbs.	1,580
Carronade	2'2"	4.4"	660 lbs.	1 lbs	870

*(from *Sink or be Sunk*, La Violette, 2002)

A typical long cannon could fire nearly a mile, whereas an equivalent carronade's effective range was less than half that. In the coming action there was more involved in scoring a hit on a target than just the range. There was the strategic use of the two guns.

The carronades on the British launches could not effectively begin to fire their guns at the *General Armstrong* until the distance between the launches and the vessel was essentially halved. By that time, the launches would have been under heavy fire from the American long cannon for almost ten minutes.

This advantage was somewhat offset by the fact that solid shot used during this period was not accurate (hence the desire to get as close as possible to your opponent).

As a result of this inherent inaccuracy, none of the solid shot fired by *General Armstrong* scored a direct hit on any of the British launches in the upcoming midnight action.

In essence, the two type guns may be compared to a rifle and a shotgun. The shotgun, or in this case the carronade, is best used in close work where accuracy is not important, and the rifle, or in this case, the long cannon, is best used in firing at a distance when hitting power is more important.

Since Reid had to consider whether to use solid or grape for the various actions that were about to take place, a word or two about these shots may be useful to explain what happens when they are fired.

Grape or grapeshot is a type of anti-personnel ammunition used by both types of cannon. Instead of a solid ball or shot, a large amount of small metal balls are tightly loaded into a canvas bag (the bag, as illustrated on the opposite page, resembles a cluster of grapes, hence the name).

On firing, the bagged grapeshot is released at high velocity from the muzzle of the gun. Almost immediately, the comparatively flimsy bag breaks open and the now released balls fan out.

The effect is similar to that of a shotgun, but in this case, the number of balls and the damage they cause is considerably more devastating.

Because of their dispersion rate and the quick loss of inertial energy, grapeshot is most devastating at short, rather than long range.

However, with the gun set at maximum elevation, it does increase its range of effectiveness, producing a widespread shower of murderous balls that can rain havoc on any exposed enemy below.

The advantage, of course, is in the wide area covered by the dispersed small shot and the longer period before the shot are released. Although the range of such devastation is somewhat short, the rain of these pellets can do a great deal of damage to men exposed below the shot.

Canister (or case-shot) is another kind of anti-personnel ammunition, similar to grapeshot, used in both types of cannon of the period. Canister consists of a closed, cylindrical, metal can typically filled with round iron balls, normally packed with sawdust to add more solidity to the mass and to prevent the balls from crowding each other when the round is fired.

The canister itself is usually made of tin dipped in a lacquer of beeswax to prevent saltwater corrosion. Iron is often substituted for tin for use in large-caliber guns, although the unit is still dipped in beeswax to increase the round's shelf life at sea.

The ends of the canister are closed with wooden or metal disks. This 'sabot' (shoe) of wood, metal, or similar material helps holds back the escaping gases and guides the round during its firing from the cannon.

Attached to the back of the metal canister is a cloth cartridge bag, which contains the round's gunpowder charge. This is pricked when the round is loaded and this is where the gunner applies his slow match.

A Naval Incident at Horta

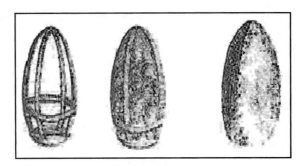

Examples of different canister cases

Attached to the back of the metal canister is a cloth cartridge bag, which contains the round's gunpowder charge. This is pricked when the round is loaded and this is where the gunner applies his slow match.

hen fired, the canister disintegrates in flight and its shards and projectiles spread out in a conical formation, causing a wide swath of destruction.

The advantage of using canister over grapeshot is that the shot is somewhat better controlled since the canister disintegrates at a greater range from the muzzle of the gun and the shot remains somewhat more concentrated.

It is also possible to fire extremely lethal double canister, or grapeshot, wherein two rounds are loaded into the cannon and then fired simultaneously using a single or double powder charge according to the range desired. Triple canister is also possible with reduced gunpowder charges for extreme close range devastation.

There is some indication that another, more subtle type of canister shot was used in the midnight action by the *General Armstrong*. This was a type of shot called *langrage,* which consisted of a cloth bag or container filled with jagged pieces of irregularly shaped iron or even, at times, broken glass.

Langrage was normally used to shred the sails of an opposing vessel or clear a deck of defenders prior to boarding. In both cases, the use of langrage was most effective.

The British later complained that the injuries of some of the wounded found in the boats of the midnight action indicated they had been hit by langrage shot.

Although not used in the midnight action, double round ball can be used by either of the two types of cannon.

The actions in the first two Horta encounters were more personnel-oriented, rather than that of banging the hull of a nearby enemy vessel and thus double solid shot was not called for. The problem with these increased rounds per shot is they lack the punch of a single round.

In Chapter 8, when Reid's intention is not directed at personnel, but rather the hull of the *Carnation*, he turns to the full punching power of the solid rounds fired by Long Tom. As will be seen, the solid rounds were effective in doing this.

"Night battle of Privateer Brig General Armstrong *of New York," oil by Emanuel Leutze*

A Naval Incident at Horta

Chapter 6

THE SECOND ACTION, MIDNIGHT, 26 SEPTEMBER

In his report in answer to a query of Commodore Lloyd as to why he did not close on the General Armstrong in the second action described here, Captain Bentham described his actions leading up to the midnight attack on the privateer as follows:

> ... proceedings from the time I received your orders (which to the best of my knowledge was about 8 o'clock p.m.) to get H.M.'s Sloop (sic *Carnation*) under my command alongside the American Privateer *General Armstrong*, and destroy her, with the boats of the *Plantagenet* and *Rota* under my command, to assist in towing or anything else circumstances might require, together with my reasons why the sloop could not be alongside the Privateer before the boats made the attack ...

The moment I received your orders, the Schooner was reported under weigh, and considerably in shore of us. The Cable of H.M.'s Sloop was immediately cut, and all sail made. Lieut. Zanssek who brought the orders was at this time alongside of us, and had repeatedly asked me if he should shove off, and other Boats were coming to support him.

I consented, and sent my Gig as a further protection, imagining the Schooner intended pushing out, and that they would be the means of retarding her until we got alongside,

... before we could gather sufficient way, to go about, the Enemy had got well in shore, light baffling winds and a strong S.W. current, prevented our closing with them although every exertion was made, before all the boats rendezvous' round us; I then, seeing the Schooner close in under the Portuguese Battery, sent my First Lieut. to you for instructions relative to the attack, and should the Batteries interfere on his return with orders to bring her out.

Lt. Matterface, senior officer, in the Boats, brought alongside of us a Boat with a letter from the Portuguese Governor with which I sent him to you.

On his return he was proceeding to join the Boats which had collected in shore, when I hailed him, asking what orders, he replied, we are to bring her out Sir, and immediately joined the Boats and commenced the attack.

It was my opinion, as well as the officers about me, that it was impossible to take a proper position in the night, without extreme risk of getting on the Rocks, and endangering the loss of H.M.'s Sloop.

I therefore did not judge it prudent to attempt being towed in, in the boats. I conceived eleven (sic) boats fully adequate to her capture and attribute the failure to the Enemy's being so to the Rocks, that the boats could not succeed in getting inside of her. ..

And so essentially ends the cautious involvement of Commander Bentham in the midnight attack. Let us leave him and return to the action's start where Lt. William Matterface sits in the midst of the milling boats completely frustrated by Bentham's waffling. It was an inauspicious start to what Matterface and the men in the launches were preparing to do.

Matterface was there because his Captain, Post-Captain Philip Somerville of *Rota*, on hearing of the earlier evening action involving the *Carnation's* boats, had sent Matterface to Commodore Lloyd to inform him that *Rota* was ready to execute any retaliatory action.

Evidently pleased by this, Lloyd placed Matterface in charge of the boat attack. However, because of his seniority, Captain Bentham, was still designated as being in overall charge of the attack. Matterface in effect had to wait on Bentham to start the action.

So as things stood, Matterface, anxiously sat in his boat waiting on Bentham, who, in turn, according to his own accounts, was waiting for a favorable wind.

There is a question of how many launches were involved. According to *Rota's* log, Matterface's group of seven *Rota* launches formed almost two thirds of the attacking force. Besides his group, there was a slightly smaller group of four launches led by Lt. Downbank of *Plantagenet*. There was one more launch. In his log, Bentham states he later added a cutter "manned and armed" to the attack force.

If we therefore accept twelve launches as the number of boats in the attack group, then between 360 and 480 men milled about the rocks in the attacking force. Most of the boats carried a 12-pound carronade in their bows, and the number in each attacking boat included, as part of the attack force, a small gun crew to fire the carronade.

By any account, it was an impressive gathering and obviously meant to be a full press action against the American privateer. The boats themselves were large launches purposely carried as standard equipment by most British warships for attacks such as this.

Night boat actions were common assault techniques used by the British Navy during this period with a great deal of success and something Matterface and the men in his launch were accustomed to doing. Captain Reid's father, it might be remembered, was captured in a British night boat action in New London during the Revolutionary War.

To put in perspective what happened in this particular action, however, it is important to emphasis that the launches in this assault had depleted the small squadron of almost all its boats, certainly all of those of *Rota* and *Carnation*.

Equally important to note is that the large number of men required for the action, had similarly depleted the squadron's vessels of much of their officers and crews. If nothing else but for the number of launches and the men in the attack force, this was a major assault.

Let us return to Lt. Matterface, the boats milling about the submerged rocks, and Bentham waiting for his wind.

About this time a Portuguese boat came from shore and gave Matterface a letter from the governor addressed to Commodore Lloyd. Matterface accepted the letter and then, hailing the *Carnation*, informed Bentham of the letter. Bentham, thereupon, ordered Matterface to row to *Plantagenet* and deliver it to Lloyd.

When Matterface arrived at the flagship and gave the note to an impatient Lloyd and, in answer to Lloyd questions, tried to tactfully explain the attack's delay, Lloyd became infuriated. He wrote a quick, angry reply for Matterface to give to the governor's envoy and ordered him to return to the rocks and for him, i.e., Lt. Matterface, to immediately commence the attack with or without *Carnation*.

Climbing back into his launch, Matterface breathed a sigh of relief. With these direct orders, he knew at last what course of action to take; the waiting was over. He urged his coxswain to hurry and the launch headed back to the rocks and the milling boats.

Once there, he shouted Lloyd's new orders to the anxious Bentham plainly visible on the *Carnation*, gave Commodore Lloyd's written reply to the envoy waiting in the Portuguese boat, and then, signaled the two officers in charge of the other two attack units to commence their attack. The officers acknowledged his signal, and the boats began to move.

The second attack had started.

When the other boats moved, Matterface motioned for his coxswain to do the same. The rowers pulled on their oars and Matterface's launch joined the others in moving from behind their rock cover. In moments, his boat was clear and headed toward the target.

As Matterface stood in his boat beside his coxswain, nothing in the moonlit scene seemed real. All around him were the other boats, moving in a long line, their oars flashing in the moonlight; the normally bright uniforms of the marines, who were part of each boat's complement, were muted carmine smudges.

Behind them, a seemingly long distance away, perfectly still in the bay's quiet waters, sat *Plantagenet* and *Rota*. In front of them, *General Armstrong* stood large against the Portuguese fort; a grim presence, waiting in complete, menacing silence.

It all seemed to have the appearance of a painting, each part of the scene painted in exquisite detail, each part mutely lit by the suffused light of the full moon. Occupying the center of the painting, the launches moved through dark water over a still, dark sea.

For a moment after clearing the rocks, there was no noise but the soft slap, slap of the long oars. Then a large dart of flame erupted from *General Armstrong's* dark shadow and, almost immediately, a tremendous crack as the sound of the American's immense 42-pounder reached them, ripping open the stillness.

There followed a brief quiet, then Lt. Matterface saw a tall, clean, white plume rise out of the water as the ball landed just short of the advancing boats.

When the plume collapsed, the scene seemed to return to what it had been before, with just the boats moving swiftly through the water; nothing else, just the boats in the moonlit water and the sweeping action of their oars.

But it was not the same.

With that single shot, the tension in the launches was gone. In the length of the long launch before him, Matterface saw broad grins on the faces of the men. It was part of the rush they all felt when a battle started, but it was a good feeling, and he realized he felt it as well.

The change was also felt by every one of the men rowing in the other launches and there arose from these a loud, simultaneous cheer, and then, led on by their officers, this was repeated three more times.

A Naval Incident at Horta

It appeared to Matterface that they had begun to move more swiftly through the water than they had before. Around him, the other boats seemed to have increased their speed as well, and to him it was as if the entire attacking force was almost being hurled toward the dark, waiting form of the *General Armstrong*.

Around the men in his launch, fixed to the bulwark so as to be as much out of the way as possible, were the men's cutlasses. In the bow, coiled neatly beside the carronade, was a grapnel, ready to be thrown up into *General Armstrong's* netting so as to firmly tie the launch to the vessel and give the men a purchase to board. A similar grapnel lay neatly coiled a short distance from Matterface near the boat's coxswain.

It was a set up honed by experience, something the men had done before and, if they lived after tonight's action, they would do again; this was to them a way of life.

This and Opposite Page) Watercolors of a War of 1812 boat attack. (Courtesy The Mariners' Museum Newport News Naval Archives, watercolor, 1840, artist unknown)

It was a way of life to Matterface as well and, while his practiced eyed professionally checked the launch's preparation as he stood beside the coxswain at the stern, swaying in time to the rhythmic movement of the launch, he felt the strong internal rush of the moment.

It was indeed, a way of life.

Suddenly, with a loud, heavy bang, the privateer's 42-pounder went off again and then, after a long pause, again. Like a metronome keeping time to the assault, the gun began a rhythmic firing, a shot going off to a time of slightly less than three minutes.

A 42-pound iron ball landed just beside one of the advancing boats drenching every one of its crew with water. Another near miss landed overly close to another launch and smashed several oars.

The launch, dead in the water, swiveled in place as the men hurriedly moved about to replace smashed oars and injured rowers. In moments, the launch was moving again, although somewhat slower.

Although the range to the British launches was still a little long, after the third firing of the 42-pounder, the American 9-pounders began firing.

In the dark shadow that was the *General Armstrong,* spurts of red flame darted forth, marking the various positions of the 9-pounders on the privateer. Plumes of water rose as their comparatively smaller balls landed in scattered fashion in front of the boats.

While the 9-pound shots were initially short, their plumes began erupting a bit nearer to the oncoming boats as they advanced, so that soon the boats flew over splash areas where shots had fallen.

Although some shot came near to swamping one or two of the launches, none of the solid shot damaged any of the boats seriously enough to cause them to sink.

Still they raced on.

In front of them, cannon smoke now completely obscured the silhouette of the *General Armstrong*; even the parapet of the old fort, at times, became completely hidden. Every so often, the smoke would billow apart as one or another of the privateer's guns fired, emitting bright orange, continuous darting flashes of light and always seemingly nonstop noise.

Then the Americans abruptly shifted from firing cannon balls to firing canister shot. As the comparatively small balls released by the canisters flew over the boats, it seemed as if some mischievous child had thrown handfuls of gravel at them. But the balls were not gravel, but heavy lead shot and injuries began occurring with fair regularity among the British attackers.

One canister burst over Matterface's launch and in the lethal rain of shot that followed, several men near the bow screamed. The men there signaled that three had been wounded and Matterface acknowledged. There was nothing he could do except make the launch go faster, and this he could not do.

The gun crews in the launches were eager to fire their own carronades and one or two of the boats did fire despite the fact that the *General Armstrong* was a good ways out of range. As Matterface watched these premature firings, he slowly became aware of a serious problem with these guns that had not been anticipated during the earlier planning meetings of the multi–boat attack.

With this long line of boats converging as they were to the one, mostly obscured, target, the boats behind the several leading boats could not fire their carronades. If they did, there was a chance their shot would hit men in the launches directly ahead of them.

This was made even more serious by the fact that the launch carronades had no solid shot to fire. The ammo for the launch guns had been deliberately limited to grapeshot.

This was Commodore Lloyd's doing.

Detail of a Nathaniel Currier print of the second action (See pages 120-121)

Lloyd had emphasized, before the attack, that he did not want the *General Armstrong* damaged. The carronades, therefore, were to fire grape so as to do the most damage to the crew of the *General Armstrong* and almost none to the privateer. Now this limitation restricted any firing to just those boats in the van.

The danger worked the reverse for the Americans. All of the *General Armstrong* 9-pounders now fired grape and canisters and any single shot, while not sinking any of the boats, scored hits on the men in the launches.

The only thing saving the attackers from complete disaster was that the Americans had difficulty in aiming their shots because of the smoke from their own guns.

With these opposing problems in mind, Matterface frantically waved trying to attract Lt. Downbank in the *Plantagenet* group of boats. Fortunately, Downbank saw him. Matterface pointed in the direction of the bow of the *General Armstrong*, indicating that Downbank should marshal his group of boats and attack there, while he would head for the privateer's stern.

Downbank waved acknowledgement and had his unit change the angle of their attack so as to converge on the *General Armstrong's* bow.

Meanwhile, the middle group of boats, consisting of a mix of *Carnation* and *Rota* launches under a *Carnation* lieutenant, headed directly at the *General Armstrong's* waist. This group was soon hammered by a virtual rain of grape from the privateer's center cannon.

One of these boats, after getting hit by one enormous point-blank shot of what must have been a double charge of grape, stopped short in water. It was seen drifting away from the vessel, moving aimlessly toward the shore with no movement discernable inside.

These were the final shots from the privateer's guns and, as the other boats in the same group reached the side of the *General Armstrong,* her gun ports slammed shut and the privateer's crew stood and, depressing several swivel guns lined along the rail, fired scatter shot directly into the boats.

At this same time, Downbank, gaining the bow of the *Armstrong*, led his group up, cutting at the netting, with the cry, "Up and board, my lads — No Quarter!" This cry of "no quarter" was repeated again and again by other British boarders as they hurled themselves at the black leather-capped crew of the privateer.

While the situation was without question desperate for all of the men involved, the cry "no quarter" by the British attackers infuriated the Americans and, as we will see, may well have led to the obvious lack of pity in the treatment of the retreating British at the end of this second action.

Matterface's launch was at this time at the *General Armstrong's* stern. The launch's oarsmen pressed hard on their oars for one final surge, and the large launch slammed into the side of the vessel with a crash that knocked Lt. Matterface and some of the standing marines off their feet.

There was a momentary scramble as men reached for grappling hooks and, in seconds, these were flung through the air and, tangling with the netting and railing, secured the boat to the side of the vessel.

With this, the launch's total complement of sailors and marines quickly clambered up the side of the privateer, cutting with cutlasses and short knives at the netting, firing their pistols and blunderbusses, and being cut down, in turn, by the return fire of the *General Armstrong's* men.

By now, Matterface was up and climbing the side of the privateer. On reaching deck level, he saw someone, obviously one of the privateer's officers standing with just a white shirt on, urging the gun crew about him to beat back the boarders.

One of the attacking crewmen climbed up beside Matterface and slashed at the netting impeding their getting on the privateer's deck. Just as the netting sliced open, a pistol shot hit the crewman and he fell backward to land in the water beside the launch.

Matterface, using the large hole the fallen seaman had managed to cut, pushed through the netting and leaped on deck, waving his cutlass, yelling for the other attackers to follow him.

The white bloused officer near the gun was also armed with a cutlass. When he saw Matterface coming aboard through the netting, he left the gun and came at him and in seconds the two were fighting among a growing melee.

***

A Naval Incident at Horta

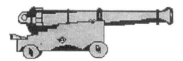

Aboard the *General Armstrong*, the second action of the night had begun an hour earlier with a warning cry from one of the lookouts.

"Deck there! They're moving out from the rocks!"

With this, the privateer crew began making final adjustments to their defenses. Reid then stood at the rail and watched the launches emerge from behind the semi-submerged rocks.

As soon as he was satisfied that the last of the British boats was clear, he ran back to the gun and pressed the slow match to the gun's priming. There was a momentary hiss, and then the gun roared and bucked backward on its restraints.

Immediately there was a sharp spit of flame accompanied by a tremendous billowing of smoke as the heavy ball raced through the air at the oncoming British.

Reid ran to the railing and, grasping the shrouds, watched to see where the ball landed. The smoke impaired his ability to see clearly, but, after a moment, he saw the ball's collapsing splash well ahead of the launches.

With the water's collapse, he heard as well, the distant cheers of the British men in the launches. Behind Reid, the gun crew had reloaded the gun, and he ran back to fire it once again, yelling for the marines in the fighting top to take over spotting the splash of the balls.

This they did as the gun went off again and then, again. However, as Reid listened to their calls, it became apparent the targets were too small to hit with the accuracy inherent in the gun's round shot. A few close misses were as close as the rounds got.

Still, there was little Reid could do except to keep firing and hoping that at least one of Long Tom's shots would score. Just one hit by one of the gun's 42-pound balls would eliminate a boat and its large crew from the engagement. Even a near miss would be disastrous to a launch.

Paul Estronza La Violette

A Naval Incident at Horta

A circa 1830 Nathaniel Currier print of the second action. It should be kept in mind that the actual action took place at night. The original print has been reversed to a mirror image to show the correct orientation of the units involved. Note the Portuguese fort is thus, correctly positioned to the left of the General Armstrong.

When the 9-pounders opened up a short time later, it became obvious, they had the same difficulty as the 42-pounder in hitting any of the oncoming boats with their solid shot.

One difficulty that plagued all of the guns was the smoke from their firing. While there was some breeze, it was so light and contrary that the smoke discharged from any of the nine guns stayed in place, screening its gun crew as well as other gun crews from seeing their targets. Again the marines in the fighting tops took over the calling of where the rounds landed among the oncoming launches.

Even with this help and when the smoke parted enough for the gun crews to see, they had trouble spotting their own shot. With the exception of the largest plumes generated by the Long Tom's shot, they could not tell which of the numerous plumes were from which gun.

Seeing this and the trouble they were having hitting the boats with solid shot, Reid quickly passed the word to the gun crews to switch from solid shot to canister. With this type ammunition being fired, accuracy was no longer a factor. The spread from each canister's discharge would cover a broad area and thus have a better chance of doing damage.

This the men at the guns did, and the results were immediately obvious to the marines spotting the calls, and this news was joyfully shouted down to the men at the guns.

The vessel soon became one almost continuous sheet of fire; the red glare of each gun's firing pierced the enveloping smoke. When a gun went off, the gun crew darted forward, swabbed the barrel clean, loaded powder, wadding and canister, and rammed it all home. Then, pulling on the gun's tackle lines, the crew rolled the weapon forward to the gun port, primed and ready to be fired again.

This was done again and again. It was as if the men were part of a complex dance; each of their individual motions were fluid, each man moving in and out of the all pervading smoke with almost ballet-like grace. The night scene resembled a gross caricature of Dante's inferno.

Still, there was a certain amount of time needed to fire each gun. Each reloading of the 9-pounders took approximately two minutes and, during each two-minute interval, the British boats, pushed hard by their officers and oarsmen, were that much closer.

The fact that the guns were being fired independently of each other, each going off as fast as each crew could clean, load and fire, helped diminish the effect of the two-minute intervals. Thus, it seemed as if at least one of the privateer's seven guns was going off at any single moment and the noise generated was almost continuous.

The lead British boats fired their carronades at the *General Armstrong* as well. The gun crews heard their shot hit above them, each hit followed by a shower of splinters and sparks where the grape hit wood or metal, soft thuds and the tinny clink belying the deadly impact of the small balls.

Then the British attackers were alongside; their boats thumping against the *General Armstrong's* hull. With this, the *Armstrong's* gun ports were slammed shut and the gun crews seized their muskets, boarding pikes, blunderbusses, and cutlasses and prepared to repel boarders.

Soon shrieks and yells, orders and oaths, amid the clang of cutlasses, were heard, coupled with the roar of small arms from the men in the tops. The bright moon and the dark smoke from the last gun firing drifted in and out of the bizarre scene, adding to the confusion.

Again and again, the enemy, led by their officers, attempted to climb the sides of the ship, cutting through the netting and gaining the deck of the privateer, but each time they were repulsed by the frenzied efforts of the *General Armstrong* crew, and the British attackers would fall back with heavy losses.

Making a desperate effort to board the bow, the British attackers finally gained the spritsail yard and bowsprit of the *General Armstrong*, and soon gained possession of the privateer's bow. With this small claw hold, they pressed their way back toward the privateer's midsection.

The American crew fought them every step, trying to stop their advance. In this turmoil, *General Armstrong's* second lieutenant, Lt. Williams, was killed and the ship's third lieutenant, Lt. Johnson, fell seriously wounded.

Meanwhile, at the ship's after section, Captain Reid was engaged in beating off the boarders coming up the side from two of the British attack boats.

The attackers were unrelenting. A broad gap was slashed in the boarding netting. Despite that the attacker responsible was shot, the gap allowed other boarders to gain the privateer's deck.

In the close action that followed, Reid found himself engaged in a hand-to-hand fight with the officer leading the British attacking force.

This officer, making a feint, brought his cutlass down with a hard blow on Reid's head. Reid had just enough time to block the blow, but still got cut across his head and nearly severed his thumb and forefinger in the process. Then, before the officer could recover, Reid slashed him with his cutlass and the lieutenant, mortally wounded, staggered and then fell back over the railing into an almost empty launch.

As others of the *General Armstrong* crew succeeded in beating off the attackers at the stern, Reid realized the firing had slackened on the forecastle. One man in the forward division ran back to report the loss of Reid's remaining two officers. With this, Reid rallied the whole of the after division about him and rushed forward.

There they met the British boarders head on just aft of the bow. For a moment, the British advance held and then, faced with the heavy pressure of the two combined divisions, the British were forced to fall back to the bow and finally, in bloody confusion, back down into their boats.

Using muskets and the swivel guns mounted on the railing, the privateer crew fired into the teeming mass of men screaming in confusion and trying desperately to push their boats away from the vessel using oars and boathooks.

Reid pressed the action, ordering the men who found themselves without cartridges, to heave cold shot into the boats in an effort to sink them,

As the British finally pulled away from the ship, the *General Armstrong* gun crews reopened their gun ports and fired their long guns, loaded with grape, into the wretched men in the retreating boats.

The cry of "no quarter" was being rewarded in a deadly way and in these last bloody moments, the second British attack of the night on the *General Armstrong* ended.

***

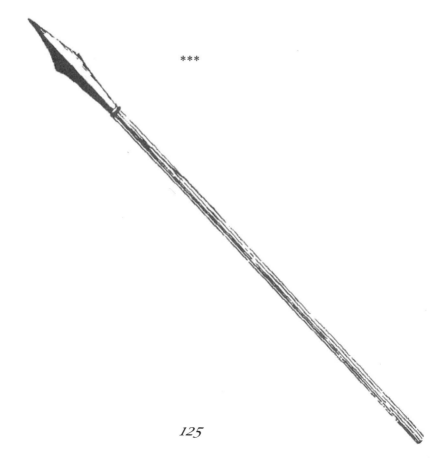

Governor Elias Jose Riberiro witnessed the second attack from the shore. Faced with an escalating situation, the intimidating presence of the large British warships, the rude reply to his earlier message to Lloyd, and the blatant fact that he could do nothing to stop what was taking place, the governor found he was at an impasse.

He sent the letter below to Lloyd immediately following the midnight attack. It is of particular interest in that he states unequivocally that the early evening action had been initiated by the British. It is written statements such as this official letter that give credence to the fact that Lloyd was the instigator of the Horta actions.

FAYAL, September 27th. 1814, 1 o'clock P. M.

TO THE COMMANDER OF THE BRITISH NAVAL FORCE IN THIS PORT:

Sir, — I received your letter, and by it I see the motives, which induce you to violate the neutrality of this port, in the contest now existing between his Britannic Majesty and the United States of America. They have been sufficiently demonstrated by the results, and I now look with alarm at those, which may follow.

I must however assure you sir, from the accounts I have received, it is certain that the British boats were the first to attack the American schooner.

I foresee fatal consequences from the sad occurrences which I have just witnessed and you sir, should therefore, now give public evidence of the harmony, friendship, alliance, and good understanding which exists between your sovereign and the Prince Regent of Portugal, by putting an end to the hostilities begun at eight o'clock this night past. Sic. &c.

ELIAS JOSE RIBERIRO

A Naval Incident at Horta

Paul Estronza La Violette

*Detail of the Nathaniel Currier print of the second action
(See page 120-121)*

Chapter 7

MIDNIGHT THROUGH DAWN, 27 SEPTEMBER

Reid stood in the waist of the now bizarrely still ship. It was true there was the moaning of the wounded, but after the noise of the cannon, the bang of the musketry and the yells and screams of the men fighting and dying, the scene about him was strangely quiet.

The deck was in great confusion. It wasn't just the spars, blocks, and cordage that had crashed through the splinter netting; there was the dead and wounded, and as he walked, the deck was slippery with human blood.

The incredible horror of the scene extended beyond the deck of the privateer. Although some of the British boats had sunk, two large launches belonging to the *Rota*, lay tied to the *General Armstrong's* stern, tied there by their now dead British attackers.

Two boats drifted a short distance away from the bow, one loaded with the dark, still bodies of British dead and in the other, it appeared that all but four of the men were dead. Some boats had drifted or were rowed ashore by three or four survivors. These boats could be seen from the deck to be full of dead bodies.

In the water, several bodies were seen draped on a bit of floating wreckage. More had washed up on the rocks in front of the fort. Several of these stood up for a moment and then fell down.

The total action that generated this grisly scene had lasted less than an hour. In that time, the large British attack force, estimated by Reid to have had about four hundred men, had been decimated.

In his final report, Lloyd acknowledges casualties in this attack alone of two hundred fifty: one hundred twenty killed and one hundred thirty wounded. Even if we accept this lesser number as accurate, the count is staggering. By any account, it was a tragic waste considering what little the attack had accomplished.

Reid's crew had also suffered. In the night's two actions, he had lost two dead and seven seriously wounded. It was an extraordinarily small number compared to the British losses, but Reid had sustained losses and to him they were not minor. In the coming action, he would miss the help that his slain and wounded officers would have provided.

Now in the moonlit semi-darkness of the post-action period, Reid had the deck of the *General Armstrong* hosed down, the wreckage of downed spars, yards, and blocks removed, and the vessel in general cleared.

There would be, he knew, more action to come. He had to clear the ship and be prepared.

Using one of the empty British launches to ferry the badly wounded (including many of the wounded British attackers), Reid went ashore on the mole on the south side of the fort where wagons sent by Dabney waited.

Once ashore, Reid sorted those he could spare among the walking wounded to act as caretakers. Like him, many of the crew had minor wounds (his hand had already started to throb.) They were certainly all exhausted. As he worked with the men, Reid received a note from the American Consul:

> Captain Reid,
> Dear Sir: You have performed a most brilliant action in beating off fourteen boats of the British ships in this road. They say they will carry the brig, cost what it will, and that the English brig will haul close in to attack you at the same time the boats do.
> My dear fellow, do not uselessly expose yourself, if again attacked by an overwhelming force, but scuttle the brig near the beach and come on shore with your brave crew.
>
> Yours truly,
> J. B. Dabney.

As Reid read the note, Dabney, himself came up and the two talked on what he should do. Reid was determined to fight, despite the fact that what lay ahead would be more difficult than what they had just been through. He told Dabney he estimated the next attack would come an hour or two after dawn when the onshore wind commenced.

Dabney repeated his advice for Reid to retire with his men ashore. Reid shook his head. He wanted to see the end, fighting with what he could. With this, the two parted and Reid returned to the ship.

He had a lot to do.

It would be impossible to repeat another defense at the same scale as they had just done. Worst of all, this time it would be *Carnation* coming in pressed by the morning's onshore wind. And she would be using her eighteen large carronades

Reid had to set up a defense aimed specifically at *Carnation*. He began formulating plans for the new action. Soon he walked about the vessel, giving orders and preparing the men and vessel for a strategy that might work and, in truth, was his only hope.

As he walked about, he found the morale of the men was good, but somber. They had just been through a terrible ordeal and were well aware a new attack was coming. The fact that they had hurled back, with heavy loss, mariners who were considered the best naval fighters in the world, gave them an inner surety: however, every man standing on the deck of the privateer knew it was not over.

What was unusual about this was that Reid and his men did not have to continue their fight: they had nothing to gain by continuing.

Honor, if that was what was wanted, was already theirs. By all accounts, they had made a superb stand against a vastly superior force. There would be no dishonor in setting fire to the vessel and retreating into the town.

Apparently Reid did not want to do this, and, as he walked and talked with the waiting men, it seemed that most did not want to do this as well.

His inspection showed that the *General Armstrong*'s damage was largely superficial, owing mainly to the British use of grapeshot. Once again it appeared the British aim had been to harm as many of the American crew as possible, while doing the least damage to their vessel.

Most importantly, his assessment showed that all six of the 9-pound long cannon were in good shape. The 42-pounder was damaged, but this was superficial. It had been upset from its carriage at its last firing just as the British boats were within yards of the *General Armstrong*. Close examination showed it had suffered no real damage, and he had it remounted and placed in a way that it would be available for any new action. With this, he found his battery of long cannon was as it was when the midnight action started.

A Naval Incident at Horta

Basically, Reid knew that if there was to be another fight, it would have to be a fight that was agreeable with the men. They had to be shown their chances were slight, but that there was a chance.

He called for all hands to muster at the waist.

***

With the midnight action the American and British accounts begin to sharply differ. As mentioned earlier, there are sufficient witnesses to the events to believe Reid's account to be the more accurate of the two. In fact, one observer onshore remarked that what happened was "as if Commodore Lloyd had stuck his hand in a jar of hornets and refused to take his hand out."

However, there are differences that indicate a partiality on the American's rendition of events. The number of boats in the British attack force is a good example; the estimation used here of there being twelve is probably more accurate than the claim of several Americans that there were fourteen.

Also, there are remarks in *Carnation*'s log that indicate an oddity in the account of the midnight action that appear to be true, but are not picked up by Reid or the two Dabney's accounts. In *Carnation*'s log there is a report of muskets firing on the attacking British boats from the rocks to the south of the *General Armstrong:*

> …a heavy firing of musketry (illegible) at some distance (ill.) from the schooner, apparently from some rocks under the battery. We did not fire on them owing to the fear of killing or wounding some of the inhabitants

133

If such firing did occur (and there is no reason to doubt the entry) and there is no report of it from Reid or the Dabneys, there is the question of who did the shooting.

It seems likely that at least some of the thirty-two American seamen Dabney reported stranded in Fayal might have been involved. He had asked the Portuguese governor to allow these seamen to go on board *General Armstrong* to help in the privateer's defense. The governor had refused.

It seems probable these same men may have borrowed muskets, positioned themselves in the rocks with these weapons and ammunition, and joined the defensive action of the *General Armstrong* on their own. If these seamen were the men firing from the rocks, their actions, of course, were a violation of the Portuguese neutrality.

On the other hand, if the men in the rocks were some of *General Armstrong's* crew, they had every right to be there, and the British had no cause to complain. Reid could put his men wherever he wished. However, as he would thus have weakened the concentration of the defenses of his ship, it is unlikely he would have placed anyone in the rocks.

No matter who the persons were doing the firing, Lloyd picked up on the *Carnation's* log entry and enlarged its importance (and location) in his report to Admiral Brown. His report makes the firing from the rocks as having a devastating effect on the British attack, if not the ultimate cause of the midnight attack's failure (the italics in his report are mine):

> But from her side being on the rocks, ... and every American in Fayal exclusive of part of the crew, being armed & concealed in these rocks, which were *immediately over the Privateer*, it unfortunately happened when these boarding men gained the deck, they were under the painful necessity of returning to their Boats, from the very destructive fire kept up *by those above them, from the shore, who were in complete security,* and I am grieved to say not before many lives were lost, exclusive of the wounded.

The account of the Horta actions by the British naval historian, Admiral William James, is even more interesting.

His account escalates the musket firing to that of a gun battery. This last is a strange and improbable statement since any such gun fire would, by the nature of grapeshot, deal more harm to the American defenders than the British attackers.

But there is more to doubt the credibility of James's account. The thought of Reid hauling a ponderous long cannon of some two thousand pounds, in the dark from the vessel to the beach, and then up to the ramparts of the fort, and doing all of this in the time he had available between the first and second attack, is really asking too much to believe.

More important, there civilians watched the action from the fort. It seems inconceivable that Reid would have the *General Armstrong* crew set up a gun battery amid a crowd of civilian onlookers.

I give Admiral William James's account of the action as an example of the Horta events that favors Commodore Lloyd's account.

However, unlike the other Horta accounts given in the Appendices, Admiral James was not there.

> …As the captain of the American privateer had now broken the neutrality of the port, Captain Lloyd determined to cut out his schooner; which had since come to again with springs close to the shore. ... at 9 p.m. four boats from the *Plantagenet* and three from the *Rota*, with about 180 seamen and marines, under the command of Lieutenant William Matterface, first of the frigate, pulled in towards the road.
>
> The *Carnation* had been directed to cover the boats in their advance; but, owing, as it appears, to the strength of the current and the intricacy of the navigation, the brig did not arrive within gun-shot of the American schooner, and therefore was not of the slightest use.

At midnight, after a fatiguing pull against a strong wind and current, the boats got within hail of the *General Armstrong*, and received from her, and from a battery erected, with a portion of her guns, on the commanding point of land under which she had anchored, a heavy fire of cannon and musketry.

In about half an hour, this fire sank two of the boats and killed or disabled two thirds of the party that had been detached in them. The remainder returned, and at about 2 a.m. on the 27th reached the *Rota*.

The loss appears to have been of the following lamentable amount: the *Rota's* first and third lieutenants (William Matterface and Charles R. Norman), one midshipman, and 31 seamen and marines killed, the *Rota's* second lieutenant (Richard Wale), First Lieutenant of marines (Thomas Park), purser (William Benge Basden), two midshipmen, and 81 seamen and marines wounded.

Among the langrage which the Americans fired, were nails, brass buttons, knife-blades, etc.; and the consequence was, that the wounded, as on former occasions recorded in this work, suffered excruciating pain before they were cured.

(Admiral William James, *Naval History of Great Britain* - Vol. VI)

A Naval Incident at Horta

A long cannon on the gun deck of a warship of the 1812 period. Note the powder boy and the short fuse being used by the officer to fire the gun. (oil, Louis-Phillippe Crepin)

Chapter 8

THE THIRD ACTION, THE SCUTTLING AND BURNING OF THE *GENERAL ARMSTRONG,*

DAWN, 27 SEPTEMBER

$\mathcal{F}$rom the several sources available, it is not clear if Commodore Lloyd ever came ashore during the squadron's stay in Horta. Judging from Commander Bentham's report, Lloyd saw the disastrous failure of the midnight attack from the deck of his flagship.

There is one source (Reid) that claims Lloyd had been injured in some way, that he had "been stepped on by an ox," but this is not verified by any reliable secondary source. Reid, in his report to his sponsors, states that "a jury of Surgeons had been held, who gave as their opinion that amputation would be necessary to insure his life."

What is important is that Commodore Lloyd may well have been in physical, as well as mental anguish, when he watched the apparent debacle of the midnight boat attack.

Later, when the full report of the attack's failure and its devastating casualty list was given by the few returning boats, he must have realized the magnitude of the tragedy his actions had generated. Despite this, he plunged ahead. It would appear Lloyd was psychologically being drawn into an ever worsening spiral from which he was unable to extract himself.

His driving energies appeared to have shifted his focus from capturing the *General Armstrong* to destroying her, no matter what the cost. He realized he could not bring *Plantagenet* or *Rota* close enough into the harbor to use their large guns. The danger to the town from errant shot would be too great. His only recourse was to use *Carnation* with its reluctant captain.

He called for his first lieutenant and gave him orders to signal *Carnation* at first light.

At dawn, Captain Bentham noted in his log a signal coming from the flag. It was #191, "engage and sink the enemy." As he watched, the signal was briefly lowered and then briskly run up once again for emphasis.

From his position on *Carnation's* quarterdeck, Bentham could see into the harbor where the first rays of the rising sun lit the *General Armstrong* lying snugly below the walls of the old fort. She looked completely unperturbed by the previous night's actions. If the vessel had looked foreboding in the moonlight, she looked even more dangerous bathed in the new day's sun.

Now, he was being told to go in and destroy her.

Turning to his First, he ordered him to beat to quarters and steer *Carnation* deeper into the harbor in the direction of the *General Armstrong*.

**

In the light of early dawn, one of the Long Tom's gun crew woke Reid, who dozed near the large gun.

He stood and looked where the man pointed across the bay toward *Carnation*. As he watched, the brig weighed anchor and began steering a course for his vessel.

Reid was a little surprised at the hour; he thought they would wait until mid-morning. There was little wind, the onshore winds had not started, and *Carnation's* movements would, at this hour, depend on the contrary between-island wind. The approach of the brig to his vessel would, as a consequence, be slow.

Well, more the better for him.

He ordered the gun crews to get ready. They had slept by their guns since the clean-up from the last of the night's two actions. There were not too many of them. Reid had stripped the vessel down to the barest crews needed to fire the guns. He didn't have to worry about repelling boarders.

Led by Dabney and with the aid of several small carriages, the men no longer needed had taken what little personal effects they had and walked beside or rode the wagons down the beach road to an old abandoned convent that sat up a short hill by a church.

There they made themselves as comfortable as they could and settled down to wait for the outcome of the day's action. The men took the precaution of taking their muskets and cutlasses with them. The Portuguese governor had said this would not be allowed, but the men insisted, and Dabney was not going to try to make them change their minds.

General Armstrong's deck had been washed down by the vessel's hoses and then heavily sanded. Thus, the blood from the previous actions had been washed away and, if there were new blood spilled in the coming action, the sand would keep it from being a problem.

Now, as the alerted crew made preparations for the oncoming *Carnation*, the privateer's gunner, Stephen Werms, walked besides each of the 9-pounders, checking its condition. He paid special attention to the port guns that had been shifted to the starboard side, making sure these guns, placed in their new positions, would not come unshipped when the guns started firing once more.

As he worked his way aft, Reid called to him. "Mr. Werms, do those guns have enough chain shot?"

"Yes, Captain. You see, we carry more chain shot than others 'cause we wanna be ready to take down the riggings of a merchant that might wanna run for it. I think we've more than enough for today. I'll check again, if you want."

"Good, do that. Also, see that the shot comes out quick on deck when things get moving,"

Reid's plan of defense was simple, and the 9-pounders' use of chain shot (i.e., two balls linked by a length of chain) played an important role in it. Unlike the previous action when he did not know whether the attack would come from, i.e., British boats or the brig, this time he knew.

It would be an unabashed direct attack by *Carnation*.

Carnation would close, firing first her two 6-pound bow chasers, and then, when within a hundred yards of *General Armstrong,* she would open up with deadly broadsides from her sixteen (eight to a side) 24-pound carronades. Once these broadsides began, Reid knew his ship was doomed.

His defenses, therefore, would depend completely on the longer range of *General Armstrong's* long cannon stopping *Carnation* before she could fire her broadsides. Now, happily, the time he had to fire these guns would be greater due to slowness of *Carnation's* approach.

If the firing of his long cannon failed to stop *Carnation,* his last act would be to scuttle the *General Armstrong* and retreat with his men, and what arms they could carry, to join the rest of the crew ashore.

He would open fire with the 42-pounder as soon as *Carnation* came within range. He and his gun crew had gone through a great deal of calculations so as to correctly elevate the gun just enough to have the heavy balls hit the hull of the British brig.

Hitting *Carnation's* hull was critical. Initially the 42-pound balls would crack the sides of *Carnation,* but as she came closer, the power behind them would increase, causing a good hit to actually hull the brig, i.e., pierce the vessel's side.

On the other hand, the six 9-pounders were angled to a much higher elevation. Firing chain shot, these guns would try to bring down *Carnation's* riggings and, with luck, some of her lesser masts. Even a slight hit to either would slow down *Carnation*. A good hit would stop her altogether. If such occurred, the brig would be forced to sit helplessly as she was hammered by the combined shot of the 42- and 9-pounders.

All of this was a far chance, but Reid was determined to try.

The *Carnation* came on, ponderously slow. She was not an exceptionally fast vessel to begin with, brigs never were, and coming in as she was, pushed by the weak wind, her movement was like a stately dowager rather than a man-of-war.

As Reid watched, she slowly, very slowly, came within the range of Long Tom. Without hesitation, he applied the slow match to the gun's touch hole.

The gun spit its large ball out with a roar.

To get a better view of where the ball would splash, Reid climbed to stand on the railing, clutching the mesh of the boarding net. It was a difficult view with the smoke from the 42-pounder whirling around him, but as he waited he realized there was no splash. He stared amazed. The round had scored on *Carnation's* hull with the first shot!

As soon as the huge gun leaped back on its tackle, the gun crew cleaned and reloaded the gun and then, tugging on the tackle, brought it back to the vessel's side. The men were well practiced in firing the huge gun and now the whole process took slightly less than three minutes.

Dropping back down to retrain the gun, Reid retouched the slow match to the gun's touch hole. Again the gun leaped in its carriage and again, Reid raced to the rail. This time there was a splash.

Carnation kept coming.

Most times, when the gun fired, there was a splash; sometimes, however, there was not, just the aftermath of a firing being a space of silence to mark the fact that a few of the 42 pound balls had landed solidly on the oncoming ship's hull.

One of these shots appeared to do exceptional damage. *Carnation* seemed to actually stop momentarily before continuing on toward the *General Armstrong*.

Soon, *Carnation* came within range of the 9-pounders, and these guns began to join in the firing.

As in the earlier boat attack, the guns were fired independently of each other, each going off as fast as each could be cleaned, loaded, and fired. The scene was that of controlled confusion. With each gun's firing, the gun would be hurled inboard, the black muzzle streaming smoke as the men threw themselves into preparing the gun for another firing.

Beneath Reid's feet, the *General Armstrong* vibrated as the ship's hull groaned and shifted. He sent one man back to check the spring-tied anchor lines, and the man returned with the word that the lines were holding.

Among the 9-pounders, the two assistant gunners ran from gun to gun, laying each at the advancing *Carnation*, firing the gun, and running to the next gun. Everywhere powder-boys ran over the wet, sand-sprinkled deck with more and more powder charges, and in the barrels beside the guns, slow matches burned.

A Naval Incident at Horta

A sketch of the Horta actions on the cover of the 1893 book written by Sam Reid's son, Samuel Reid, The Wonderful Battle of the Brig General Armstrong at Fayal, Azores 1814.

All about the ship, the men worked at their tasks, pushing themselves to make the guns go off again and again as rapidly as they could.

There was little yelling; each man worked his station, concentrating on what he did. A gun would go off, hurl back against its tackle, belching fire and smoke, and, once reloaded, it would be hauled back into position by its sweating crew and fired again.

The rapidity of the firing heated the guns so there was a danger of the guns prematurely exploding, and, running back and forth among the crews, the gunner remonstrated them of this danger. If they slowed their rate of fire as a result of this, it was difficult to tell.

145

The 9-pounders exclusively fired chain shot at *Carnation*, and it appeared that although they scored occasional hits to the vessel's masts and riggings, these appeared to be causing no serious damage.

The chain shot made a completely different sound than the hollow rush of air the round shot made or the deadly rush, like rain, small balls of canister shot made. Chain shot made a curious whirring sound, as if a covey of partridges had been startled into flight.

The very nature of this type of shot made accuracy a now and then thing, and the water about *Carnation* danced with near-hit splashes. One ball, breaking free of the chain connecting it to the other, flew on by itself, skimming flat on the surface of the water, making a sort of ducks-and-drakes passage with its numerous bounces.

But *Carnation* kept coming closer and closer. Then, deadly close, her bow chasers stopped firing and the brig started a turn so as to permit a broadside of all eight of her port side 24-pound carronades.

Reid paused in firing the 42-pounder. As he watched, the side of *Carnation* belched fire. He and every man aboard the *General Armstrong* fell to the deck. *Carnation* was firing solid shot and, when these landed, they did extensive damage. Masts, spars, and various riggings rained down on the men. Some shot hit the hull with loud, heavy slams. The privateer shuddered.

It was clear they meant to sink the *General Armstrong*. Reid decided to help them. As *Carnation* tacked to bring her starboard guns to bear, he yelled to the men in the waist to start their prearranged scuttle plan, that was that one gun be pull from its station and tilted down through an open hatch into the hull. The gun involved was one of the port guns that had been moved to the starboard side.

This work was only started when the men fell to the deck again as a second devastating broadside hit the *General Armstrong* from *Carnation's* starboard carronades. As with the first broadside, it did cruel damage.

Reid looked around at the wreck the ship was becoming. They had only a few minutes to shoot the scuttling gun and abandon the vessel before *Carnation* tacked and fired a broadside from her port carronades. Behind him, the gun crew fired Long Tom on their own and as if on cue, the several loaded 9-pounders fired as well.

There began an unusually long pause in *Carnation's* broadsides. Reid yelled at the men to pull the scuttling gun as fast as possible to the hatch. Just at the moment the scuttling gun was about to be fired, a loud cheer erupted from the other gun crews.

Reid turned to look at the *Carnation.* He stopped, amazed.

Her main topmast tottered in place, and then, with a slow twisting, then at an increasing pace, fell by the board. The *Carnation* itself was all but stopped in the water.

As the Americans watched, they were treated to an even more wondrous sight. *Carnation,* evidently so cut up in her rigging and hull that, with her guns silent, slowly turned about and began to retire.

This time the Americans did not fire their guns at the retreating British. Reid ordered a cease fire and around him, men crowded the rails to watch as *Carnation* ponderously withdrew from the action.

In the jubilant air that followed, he walked about and examined the privateer. Things were not good. *Carnation's* guns, while not causing any serious injuries to any of the gun or their crews, had done extensive damage to the vessel's frame as well as her spars and riggings. It was obvious that even if the *General Armstrong* would be permitted to do so, she would not last a day in an open sea.

At about this same time, a message was delivered to him from Dabney. It was not good news. The message stated that Commodore Lloyd had issued an unbelievable ultimatum to the Portuguese governor: the British squadron would fire on the town if the Americans were not given up.

In view of this and the condition of his ship, and the certainty of *Carnation*'s return, Reid decided he would go ahead with his plan to scuttle and abandon *General Armstrong*.

One source states Reid had the men cut down the masts and that he then used two of the 9-pounders to blow a hole through her bottom. Whatever the method he used to scuttle the vessel, the G*eneral Armstrong* sank in such a way so she could not be reasonably salvaged.

The abandoned convent (left) and church (right) of S. Francisco (Horta Municipal Archives)

This done, Reid called the crew together and, having them take what they needed from the vessel, told them they were going to retreat to the convent.

Leaving the ship resting on the bottom of the shallow waters, her decks barely awash, he and his men boarded one of the captured British boats and rowed the short distance to shore and then went to join the rest of the crew in the old convent.

***

When *Carnation* came out from her one-sided encounter with *General Armstrong*, it was quite evident she had not done well. Her main topmast was down, her bowsprit shot through, and, from the  evident change in her draft, she had been hulled in several places.

It was equally obvious to anyone who saw her that she required extensive repairs if she was to be restored to true seaworthiness. It all seemed impossible to imagine that just fifteen hours earlier, the task of cutting out the privateer as a prize seemed to be something that would be quickly and easily done. It was evident from the present state of the *Carnation* that this was not true.

The British losses in the two-day engagement were incredible by anyone's count. It appeared Commodore Lloyd's squadron so far had lost, by their own count, 120 killed, 140 wounded, including almost all of *Rota's* officers and four of *Plantagenet's* lieutenants. The squadron had lost or had damaged all their boats. And now, the crowning blow, one of the three ships in Commodore Lloyd's command was badly damaged.

(Opposite page) In April 1867, Charles Dabney gave a complete description of the rescue of the figurehead of the General Armstrong *in a letter to the Boston Naval Library and Institute.*

> ...*The morning after the extraordinary victory of Capt. Reid and his officers and crew of that vessel, over the thirteen boats, manned from the "Plantagenet," "Rota," and "Carnation," they having landed all their baggage and stores, a nine pounder was discharged down the Brig's main hatchway and she was abandoned. The water was so shallow that all above main deck was out of water. The "Carnation," Brig of war, had been brought in close and was firing grape shot at her, when the Boatswain of the G.A. (I regret that his name is not to be found where I expected), a Herculean figure, deliberately walked down, with a mate, opposite to beach where the vessel was, and declared that they (the then enemies) should not have the Figure Head. He came provided with a hatchet, swam off to the vessel about fifteen feet, gone on board, cut off the head and brought it ashore. During that time the mate waited on the beach (somewhat protected by the upper works of the vessel); on their return when running along the beach to where I was with many others protected by an angle of the Fort, the mate was seen to fall, as if mortally wounded; I immediately sent two men to take him to the Hospital, where on examination it appeared that a grape shot had cut through the muscular part of one of his arms and one had carried away a part of the calf of one of his legs; both severe but not dangerous...*

The figurehead now rests quite close to the 42-pound Long Tom in the Naval Museum in Washington, D.C.

A Naval Incident at Horta

Paul Estronza La Violette

A Naval Incident at Horta

(Above and opposite) Long Tom with several Portuguese military in place in the Forte de Santa Cruz. Although the 42-pounder went down with the ship in the mid 1800s, it was later recovered by the Portuguese and installed as a part of the arsenal of the fort's revitalization. After many years of American and Portuguese diplomatic parleys, it was returned with much ceremony to the United States.

It has now found a final resting place in the large exhibit hall of the Naval Museum in Washington, D.C.

In a towering rage, Lloyd sent a *Plantagenet* officer to personally relay an order for *Carnation* to return within pistol shot of the *General Armstrong,* to anchor there and then use the brig's cannon to destroy her.

Captain Bentham went back in as ordered and sent boarding parties to examine the scuttled ship. This took some time. When the boarding parties returned, they reported that they had found little of real value beyond souvenirs and some supplies.

Bentham then sent the *Plantagenet* boat back to Commodore Lloyd with the report that he had assessed the hulk as well as its contents and nothing of value could be salvaged. Exasperated, Lloyd sent the same boat back to Captain Bentham with specific orders: he was to immediately set fire to the wreck.

Captain Bentham at last did as he was ordered. The superstructure above water was set afire and with these actions, the *General Armstrong* was essentially destroyed.

It is here that Commodore Lloyd's final report of the affair to Rear Admiral Brown (Appendix B) becomes its most strange. The following excerpt from that report is the *entire section* that describes the final engagement of *Carnation* and *General Armstrong*:

> "Sometime after a favorable breeze sprung up, and Capt. Bentham soon anchored the brig close to the Privateer, and in a short time she was a perfect wreck & then burnt. She proved to be the noted American Privateer *General Armstrong* pierced for 18, but mounting only Eight long 9's and one long 42 pr. Guns, about 360 Tons burthen, with a complement of 90 men, out 16 days from New York, had taken nothing, fitted out and bound on nine months cruise, one of the fastest sailing vessels out of America, & is said to have taken & destroyed British property to the amount of a million Dollars on her former cruises."

In effect, Lloyd's report would leave Rear Admiral Brown and the Board of Admiralty readers with the impression that a heavy dawn engagement had *not* taken place and that *Carnation* had easily sailed to within pistol shot of the famed and most dangerous privateer, *General Armstrong,* quickly destroyed her with several broadsides, and burnt the wreckage.

Nothing, if one were to believe Lloyd's account, could have been simpler.

The guns presently in the old fort. There is good evidence these guns were some of the 9-pounders rescued from the General Armstrong *after the battle. The fort today is a hotel and a swimming pool and cabanas accompany the guns on the old fort's battlement.*

Chapter 9

AFTERMATH,

27 SEPTEMBER - 5 OCTOBER

With the sinking and burning of the *General Armstrong*, Commodore Lloyd appeared to realize that the events of the last two days could well become a setback to the direction of his career despite the British system of promotion by seniority. Yet he went on in a manner that seemed to indicate he was barely able to keep his self-control.

His entire set of actions following the destruction of the *General Armstrong* indicated a person floundering on ways to injure the Americans and, at the same time, make what he did appear in some way rational.

He did seem to realize that after what happened, it would be folly to stage a land attack on the Americans ensconced in the old convent and from reports from the shore, appeared to be armed and determined to fight.

To his Excellency the Governor of Fayal

Sir,

Having been informed that several British Subjects are among the Crew of the late American Privateer *General Armstrong* now on Shore, and that two of them in particular, formerly belonging to His Majesty's Ship *Guerriere*, where I had the Honor to command her, I am induced to request you will from the good Understanding subsisting between your Royal Master Prince Regent of Portugal and His Britannic Majesty's the above men to be given up to me as Traitors to their king and Country that they may be sent to England and tried according to the Law of Nations for their Offence.

And in Consequence of the great number of American Seamen now on Shore and from the Knowledge of their general Conduct I have not the least Doubt they will attempt to seize on some British Subject when unprotected by the Presence of His Britannic Majesty's Ships. I have to beg you will either cause them immediately to leave the Island or be put in Confinement that the above Event may be avoided. Otherwise I shall be under the Necessity of leaving one of the Ships under my Orders to cruize (sic) off this Port for the Protection of British Property and prevent American Privateers rendezvousing in the Roads.

I have the Honor to be

Sig./ Robt Lloyd Captain

Even a successful attack, if it was accompanied by heavy British casualties, would be hard to justify to Admiral Brown on the return of Lloyd and his squadron to Jamaica. As things were, his written accounts of what happened in Horta bordered on fantasy, easily discerned as such by any knowledgeable reader.

The letter opposite is an example of this. It tries to tie some of his action to an old wound, HMS *Guerriere*. He, like many British naval officers felt the loss of HMS *Guerriere* as a personal affront, he probably more so, since he had once been her captain.

What is perhaps the strangest part of the whole affair is that he describes in detail the two men he claims to be deserters. He is very emphatic that the men had been part of HMS *Guerriere's* crew and were now part of the *General Armstrong's* crew taking refuge in the convent.

Perhaps there had been two such deserters and that Lloyd knew them. But as to their being part of the *General Armstrong* crew, it appeared, to put it bluntly, just a part of Lloyd's insane desire to rationalize his actions.

Whatever the truth, he claimed the men existed and were presently in Horta. He had the letter delivered to the Portuguese governor with a strong verbal protest and insistence that the two be turned over to his officers. The events in the various accounts that followed this claim by Lloyd were confusing.

Some accounts state the Portuguese authorities went to the convent and, on reviewing the American crew, found no one answering Lloyd's description. This was so reported back to the British officers representing Lloyd.

Another account of the incident (which was also mentioned in a note of protest by Consul Dabney) indicates that several of the American crew were brought back by the Portuguese authorities to Horta City offices, where they were allowed to be reviewed by British officers. These officers, after careful examination, deemed them not to be the men described by Lloyd.

In any case, considering what had happened over the last two days and the still strong feelings remaining among the Americans from the USS *Chesapeake*/HMS *Leopard* affair, it is doubtful Reid would have given up any of the *General Armstrong* crew to Lloyd's officers.

Throughout this period, the Portuguese governor strived to maintain the port's neutrality to avoid further damage to the town. After a bit of haggling, he was successful in collecting the weapons the privateer crew brought with them to the old convent. When the British wanted to come ashore, the governor insisted they do so without weapons.

At two in the afternoon of the day of the *Carnation* action, sixty British officers and seamen, as well as a small band, were allowed to land on the mole to retrieve the wounded and bury the men killed in the preceding night's battle.

The Portuguese flag, which the governor had ordered taken down to show displeasure with the British attacks, was ordered raised in respect for the British dead. In addition, the governor wanted the ceremonies to take place without incident and sent a forty-man force to accompany the landing party and keep the Americans away from the ceremonies.

Despite this effort, two American seamen were reported to have yelled insults as the British left the funeral. These men were temporarily arrested. It was not clear, whether these men were from the *General Armstrong*.

Having buried his dead, Lloyd now busied himself with repairing the *Carnation* and preparing to continue with the sailing orders given to him by Admiral Brown, despite the fact he was deficient in officers, especially so aboard *Rota*.

In a post-engagement conversation with Consul Dabney, Post-Captain Philip Somerville of *Rota* remarked that he had lost seventy dead and wounded from his ship in the night actions (this number did not include some walking wounded who were returned to limited duty). In effect, *Rota, Plantagenet,* and *Carnation* desperately needed replacements of both officers and men.

In getting these replacements, Lloyd was lucky.

The brig, *Thaïs,* came into port three days after the actions, and her companion on patrol, the brig, *Calypso*, came in early the following day.

(It is interesting to note that according to the *Thaïs* and *Calypso* captains' logs, neither vessel was in the area of the *General Armstrong* when she exchanged gun fire with a British man-of-war on 12 September. However, while Reid's worry about *Thaïs* and *Calypso* chasing him was not based on fact, his worry did have validity since, by the purest of chance, here entering port on the very day he predicted was the first and, a day later, the second of the two warships.)

The two warships were delivered a surprised when they entered the harbor. Lloyd immediately took advantage of his broad Commodore pennant to commandeer the two vessels to use as sources of new officers to fill the vacancies in his command and as hospital vessels.

In addition, Lloyd wanted the two brigs to transport the severely wounded back to Great Britain. There is no official record of what the commanding officers of the two brigs thought of this, but Captain Mein of *Thais* is reported by Charles Dabney to have considered Commodore Lloyd a "savage madman."

A few words concerning the British wounded being transported to England might shed some light on their suffering.

Calypso sailed from Horta on 2 October, with about twenty-five of the more severely wounded. Bad weather delayed transporting the wounded to the *Thais* and, as a result, she did not sail until 4 October.

Remember that the walking wounded were returned to limited duty on their respective ships where at least they were under the care of their mates. The more serious of the injured were not as lucky.

Consider *Calypso's* trip back to England with its human cargo.

Calypso normally had a crew of 120 men. To accommodate this many men, they normally stand port and starboard watches, resulting in half the crew being on deck at any one time and half the crew below.

Less the bowsprit, the brig is slightly over 100 feet in length. The result is that, although each crewman can only sleep four hours at a time, he has full room to stretch out in his hammock below deck when he does so. Although this arrangement is not ideal, the men become accustomed to it.

Lloyd stripped *Calypso* of a goodly number of its original 120 men. Still there must have been enough crew remaining aboard to sail the vessel. If we say that Lloyd commandeered thirty men, that would leave *Calypso* with a crew of ninety men.

Since the normal off-duty watch was sixty men, the loss of fifteen men from each watch would ease the below deck normally crowded conditions

But now the *Calypso* has been entrusted with twenty-five seriously wounded who required constant care. Since any bad weather would be detrimental to their care, the twenty-five wounded must have been kept in the stifling conditions below deck.

If we consider the crowding of the off-duty watch was bad before, the fetid atmosphere generated in the crowded crew's spaces with the off-duty watch and the addition of twenty-five gravely wounded men must have been appalling.

Think about it

Calypso is headed to England, at least a good two weeks sailing away, barring bad weather (and they did have bad weather). For the wounded, the two-week trip (*Calypso* arrived at Spithead on 16 October) aboard the crowded brig cannot have been pleasant.

On another note concerning the two brigs, Lloyd did not want of what had happened in Horta to return to Great Britain before his official letters and reports. He thus ordered that no mail from the squadron be allowed to accompany either *Calypso* or *Thais* on their return to England. All mail, he ordered, was to be held until the squadron returned to Jamaica.

Since the squadron was not scheduled to return to Jamaica for almost two months, no word other than that of Lloyd's communiqué concerning the Horta actions would be received in England until then.

Even when they arrived in Jamaica, letters would still take weeks to go from there to England. As it so happened many things happened in the interval, and it appears Lloyd managed to cover his tracks fairly well.

But not completely.

Lloyd sent a letter with *Calypso* addressed to the Admiralty Board in London asking to be excused in his actions in commandeering the two brigs. It was addressed to the Admiralty Board's First Secretary, John W. Croker:

> Robert Lloyd to John W. Croker
> His Majesty's Ship *Plantagenet* Fayal Road
> 1st October 1814
> Sir,
>
> I beg leave to enclose you for the information of my Lords Commissioners of the Ministry a report of the Surgeons of His Majesty's Ships under my command, on the state of the wounded officers Seamen & Marines, belonging to His Majesty's Ships *Plantagenet* & *Rota*, in consequence of which I judged it necessary to order His Majesty's Ship *Thais* & Sloop *Calypso*, as they were nearly out of provisions to receive all the wounded from this Ship and the *Rota* which required Hospital treatment, and proceed without loss of time with them to England, which I hope their Lordships will approve of...
>
> I have the honor to be Sir Your most Obt
> Robert Lloyd Captain

Lloyd's letter didn't fool Croker one bit.

Croker had been First Secretary since 1804 and would be so until 1830. During that time, he had heard it all. Lloyd's letter and his report to Admiral Brown created dissatisfaction in Croker and members of the Admiralty Board, including the First Lord.

The following is a transcription to Commodore Lloyd from the Admiralty Board, dated 19 October 1814.

This proceeding appears to be altogether unjustifiable:

1. The sending a Boat late in the evening as it is said "to observe the proceedings" of the Privateer, was most likely to produce the effect which followed, & from the circumstances of the Vessel having been effectually "watched" during the night by other means, seems to have been wholly unnecessary.—

2. The honor & character of our Navy would not have been in the least degree impaired if with a 74 Gun Ship, a large Frigate, & three smaller Vessels, opposed to one Privateer, we had deferred till day light any hostile Measures against her, supposing such Measures to have been justifiable.

3. On the point of neutrality, the regular course, I apprehend, would have been in the first instance to complain to the Portuguese Governor. It would have been time enough to take the law into our own hands when proper redress had been refused.

4. The sending home of the *Thais* & *Calypso* instead of the *Rota* is of a piece with all the previous steps.—

The whole proceeding deserves strong animadversion.

A Naval Incident at Horta

The Old Admiralty, Whitehall, London, 1830 (old print)

In effect, the Admiralty chastised Lloyd for his conduct in the Horta action in general and voiced their displeasure of Commodore Lloyd's actions in a "neutral port" in particular. The Board was not pleased and said so.

There was more.

The following is a note that was later added to the above transcription. It is thought to be in Secretary Croker's handwriting:

> Send me copies of Capt. Lloyd's letter No. 1 & the enclosures (except the return of killed & wounded) in order that I may take measures for ascertaining what is to be done on the violation of the Neutral Port.

On 21 October, Croker's dialogue continued. The following note was added to the Admiralty Board's transcription, it also appears to be in Secretary Croker's handwriting:

> ... The Board highly disapproves of the injudicious attack of the ships boats under the orders of Captain Lloyd and further disapproves of his directing the two Sloops from the service on which they were ordered leaving that Station entirely unprotected instead of completing their provisions & sending the *Rota* home with the wounded Men –
>
> At the same time that he states the numerous privateers of the enemy being in that neighborhood ...

(I leave the reader to underline the parts in any of the above transcription which may need emphasizing. It certainly appears from this that Commodore Robert Lloyd was being given a "strong animadversion.")

Meanwhile in Horta, Captain Lloyd was still stirring the pot.

He demanded the remains of the *General Armstrong* be given to him as a prize of war, or he would take them by force. Although set afire by *Carnation,* much of the hull of the *General Armstrong* was protected from the flames when she sank in the shallow water. It would seem that Lloyd thought some of this was salvageable and, therefore, had some monetary value.

In order to avoid additional bloodshed, the local Portuguese judge, at first, wanted to let him have it. John Dabney did not think so. He vigorously expressed his opinion that whatever remains of the privateer were of value should be surrendered to him to lay a basis for a future claim against the British government.

The British Vice Consul, Mr. Parkin, and Captain Mein of the *Thais* (the same officer who considered Commodore Lloyd a "savage madman") talked at length to Dabney, trying to reach a common ground.

Finally, the three put forth the suggestion that any salvage from the *General Armstrong* be sold and the funds so derived be used to pay for repairing the buildings in the town damaged during the actions. (The *Carnation's* broadsides had caused considerable damage to the houses near the fort, as well as a number of injuries.)

The Portuguese judge agreed with this position, the governor went along with it, and it seems even Lloyd was won over to the wisdom of the idea (especially since, as stated above, much of the damages had been due to *Carnation)*.

With the British dead buried in a small cemetery just outside Horta, the *Carnation* repaired to seaworthy condition, and the wounded sent back to Great Britain aboard *Calypso* and *Thais,* Commodore Lloyd and his squadron sailed out of the Port of Horta on 5 October.

He left behind him the burnt hulk of the *General Armstrong*, resting in the shallows in front of Forte de Santa Cruz, as a grim reminder of his brief stay

Eight days after the battle, 5 October, Captain Reid and his crew sailed aboard a Portuguese brig bound for Amelia Island in Spanish Florida.

Unlike Commodore Lloyd, who left with all the ships of his squadron, the people of the *General Armstrong* embarked without their ship.

However, they did leave with the knowledge that they had fought the best they could against what was reputed to be the world's finest mariners and that their best had been extraordinarily good.

The naval incident at Horta was over.

A Naval Incident at Horta

Paul Estronza La Violette

EPILOGUE

In his 1893 book *The Wonderful Battle of the Brig General Armstrong at Fayal, Azores 1814,* Captain Samuel Chester Reid's son, Samuel Reid wrote a final and more cordial account of the battle's aftermath.

Let us close the account of the naval battle with his description of what happened:

> After it became evident that Commodore Lloyd did not intend to execute his threat to take Captain Reid and his crew prisoners, they left their quarters in the old convent and returned to the town of Horta.
>
> Several British officers, who had come ashore to attend the burial of their deceased comrades, sent a note to Captain Reid, who was then staying at the house of Consul Dabney, with the request that he would meet them at the British Consul.
>
> Mr. Dabney, who was of the opinion that it was only a ruse to arrest Captain Reid or bring about a duel, counseled him not to go.

But Reid said he did not apprehend any indignity, and not to go would be treating them with discourtesy. He accordingly dressed in full uniform, with sash and cutlass, and as he approached the quarters of the British Consul he observed a number of British officers standing in front of the house, who on recognizing him, lifted their caps and gave him a cheer, to Reid's great surprise.

On being invited to enter the house, and after the compliments of the day were passed, one of the lieutenants said, "We have desired the pleasure of your company, Captain, in order to settle a question among ourselves, as to whether or not you and your crew wore steel shirts of mail during the battle? For both our men and officers are confident that they saw our bullets strike your crew and yourself frequently, and they glanced off like hail."

Captain Reid laughed at this charge, and replied, "Why, gentlemen, I can assure you that the only steel armor that my officers and men wore was their cutlasses and steel-strapped helmets. As for myself, I admit that your bullets tickled my ears so often that I was almost afraid to turn my head.

But you saw I was in my shirt sleeves, and I pledge you, on the honor of a sailor, that the only shirt of mail I wore was a *linen* shirt, which I don't deny was *a shirt of a male!*'"

A hearty laugh followed, which ended in several bottles of wine being opened and a jolly time.

A Naval Incident at Horta

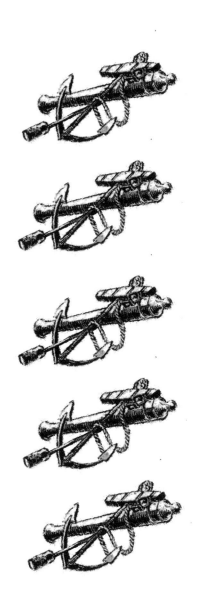

Paul Estronza La Violette

*Appendices,
Glossary
and
Acknowledgements*

Paul Estronza La Violette

Captain Samuel Chester Reid of the General Armstrong
(Oil by John Wesley Jarvis, 1815)

Appendix A:

CAPTAIN REID'S REPORT
AND
CAPTAIN REID AFTERWARD

With infinite regret I am constrained to say it has eventually fallen to my lot to state to you the loss and total destruction of the privateer brig *Gen. Armstrong*, late under my command.

We sailed from Sandy Hook on the evening of the 9th ult. and about midnight fell in close aboard of a razee and ship of the line. They pursued till next day noon, when they thought proper to give over chase.

On the 11th, after a nine hour's chase, boarded the private armed schr. *Perry*, John Colman, 6 days from Philadelphia; had thrown over all his guns.

On the following day fell in with an enemy's gun brig; exchanged a few shots with, and left him. On the 24th, boarded a Spanish brig and schooner, and a Portuguese ship, all from Havana.

On the 26th following, came to in Fayal Roads, for the purpose of filling water; called on the American Consul, who very politely ordered our water immediately sent off, it being our intention to proceed to sea early the next day.

At 5 P. M. I went on board, the consul and some other gentlemen in company. I asked some questions concerning enemy's cruisers, and was told there had been none at these Islands for several weeks; when about dusk, while we were conversing the British brig *Carnation* suddenly hove in sight close under the N. E. head of the harbor, within gunshot when first discovered.

The idea of getting under way was instantly suggested; but finding the enemy's brig had the advantage of a breeze and but little wind with us, it was thought doubtful if we should be able to get to sea without hazarding an action. I questioned the Consul to know if in his opinion the enemy would regard the neutrality of the port. He gave me to understand I might make myself perfectly easy, assuring me at the same time they would never molest us while at anchor.

But no sooner did the enemy's brig understand from the pilot-boat who we were, when she immediately hauled close in and let go her anchor within pistol shot of us. At the same moment the *Plantagenet*, and frigate *Rota*, hove in sight, to whom the *Carnation* instantly made signal, and a constant interchange took place for time.

The result was the *Carnation* proceeded to throw out all her boats; dispatched one on board the commodore, and appeared otherwise to be making unusual exertions.

From these circumstances I began to suspect their real intentions. The moon was near its full, which enabled us to observe them very minutely; and I now determined to haul in nearer the shore. Accordingly, after clearing for action we got under way, and began to sweep in. The moment this was observed by the enemy's brig, she instantly cut her cable, made sail, and dispatched four boats in pursuit of us.

Being now about 8 P.M. as soon as we saw the boats approaching, we let go our anchor, got springs on our cable, and prepared to receive them. I hailed them repeatedly as they drew near, but they felt no inclination to reply. Sure of their game, they only pulled up with the greater speed.

I observed the boats were well manned, and apparently as well armed; and as soon as they had cleverly got alongside we opened our fire, which was as soon returned; but meeting with rather a warmer reception than they had probably been aware of, they soon cried out for quarters, and hauled off.

In this skirmish I had one man killed and my First Lieutenant wounded. The enemy's loss must have been upwards of twenty killed and wounded. They had now repaired to their ships to prepare for a more formidable attack. We, in the interim, having taken the hint, prepared to haul close in to the beach, where we moored head and stern within half pistol shot of the castle.

This done, we again prepared in the best possible manner for their second reception. About 9 P.M. we observed the enemy's brig towing in a large fleet of boats. They soon left the brig and took their stations in three divisions, under covert of a small reef of rocks, within about musket shot of us. Here they continued maneuvering for some time, the brig still keeping under way to act with the boats, should we at any time attempt our escape.

The shore was lined with the inhabitants waiting the expected attack; and from the brightness of the moon, they had a most favorable view of the scene. The Governor, with most of the first people of the place, stood by and saw the whole affair.

At length about midnight, we observed the boats in motion, (our crew having laid at their quarters during the whole of this interval.) They came on in one direct line, keeping in close order; and we plainly counted twelve boats. As soon as they came within proper distance we opened our fire, which was warmly returned from the enemy's carronades and small arms.

The discharge from our Long Tom rather staggered them; but soon recovering, they gave three cheers, and came on most spiritedly. In a moment they succeeded in gaining our bow and starboard quarter, and the word was Board.

Our great guns now becoming useless, we attacked them sword in hand, together with our pikes, pistols, and musketry, from which our lads poured on them a most destructive fire.

The enemy made frequent and repeated attempts to gain our decks, but were repulsed at all times, and at all points, with the greatest slaughter. About the middle of the action I received intelligence of the death of my second Lieutenant; and soon after of the third Lieutenant being badly wounded.

From this and other causes, I found our fire had much slackened on the forecastle; and, fearful of the event, I instantly rallied the whole of our after division, who had been bravely defending and now had succeeded in beating the boats off the quarters.

They gave a shout, rushed forward, opened a fresh fire, and soon after decided the conflict, which terminated in the total defeat of the enemy, and the loss of many of their boats: two of which, belonging to the *Rota*, we took possession of, literally loaded with their own dead.

Seventeen only escaped from them both, who had swam to the shore.

In another boat under our quarter, commanded by one of the Lieutenants of the *Plantagenet*, all were killed saving four. This I have from the Lieutenant himself, who further told me that he jumped overboard to save his own life.

The duration of this action was about 40 minutes.

Our deck was now found in much confusion, our Long Tom dismounted, and several of our carriages broken; many of our crew having left the vessel, and others disabled. Under these circumstances, however, we succeeded in getting Long Tom in his berth, and the decks cleared in some sort for a fresh action, should the enemy attack us again before daylight.

About 3 A.M. I received a message from the American Consul, requesting to see me on shore, where he informed me the Governor had sent a note to Captain Lloyd, begging him to desist from further hostilities.

To which Captain Lloyd sent for answer, that he was now determined to have the privateer at the risk of knocking down the whole town; and that if the Governor suffered the Americans to injure the privateer in any manner, he should consider the place an enemy's port, and treat it accordingly.

Finding this to be the case, I considered all hopes of saving our vessel to be at an end. I therefore went on board, and ordered all our wounded and dead to be taken on shore, and the crew to save their effects as fast as possible.

Soon after this it became daylight, when the enemy's brig stood close in, and commenced a heavy fire on us with all her force. After several broadsides she hauled off, having received a shot in her hull, her rigging much cut, and her foretopmast wounded (of this I was informed by the British Consul).

She soon after came in again, and anchored close to the privateer. I then ordered the *Armstrong* to be scuttled, to prevent the enemy from getting her off. She was soon after boarded by the enemy's boats, and set on fire, which soon completed her destruction. They have destroyed a number of houses in the town, and murdered some of the inhabitants.

By what I have been able to learn from the British Consul and officers of the fleet, it appears there were about 400 officers and men in the last attack by the boats, of which 120 were killed and about 130 wounded.

Captain Lloyd, I am told by the British Consul, is badly wounded in the leg; a jury of Surgeons had been held, who gave as their opinion that amputation would be necessary to insure his life. 'Tis said, however, that the wound was occasioned by an Ox treading on him.

The fleet has remained here about a week, during which they have been principally employed in burying their dead, and taking care of their wounded.

Three days after the action they were joined by the ship *Thais* and brig *Calypso* (two sloops of war) who were immediately taken into requisition by Captain Lloyd, to take home the wounded men.

The *Calypso* sailed for England with part of the wounded, on the 2d instant, among who was the First Lieutenant of the *Plantagenet*. The *Thais* sails this evening with the remainder.

Capt. Lloyd's fleet sailed today, supposed for the West-Indies.

The loss on our part, I am happy to say is comparatively trifling; two killed and seven wounded.

With regard to my officers in general I feel the greatest satisfaction in saying they one and all fought with the most determined bravery, and to whom I feel highly indebted for their officer-like conduct during the short period we were together; their exertions and bravery deserved a better fate.

I here insert for your inspection, a list of the killed and wounded.

KILLED.
    Mr. Alexander O. Williams, 2d Lieut, by a musket ball in the forehead, died instantly;
    Burton Lloyd, Seaman, do. through the heart, do.

WOUNDED.
    Fredk. A. Worth, 1st Lieut, in the right side.
    Robert Johnson, 3d do. left knee.
    Bazilla Hammond, dr. Master, left arm.
    John Finer, Seaman, knee.
    Wm. Castle, do. Arm.
    Nicholas Scalsan, do. arm and leg.
    John Harrison, do. hands and face, by the explosion of a gun.

-

It gives me much pleasure to announce to you that our wounded are all in a fair way of recovery, through the unremitted care and attention of our worthy surgeon.

Mr. Dabney, our Consul, is a gentleman possessing every feeling of humanity, and to whom the utmost gratitude is due from us for his great care of the sick and wounded, and his polite attention to my officer and myself.

Mr. Williams was a most deserving and promising officer. His country, in him, has lost one of its brightest ornaments; and his death must be sadly lamented by all who knew his worth.

Accompanied with this you will find a copy of my Protest, together with copies of letters written by Mr. Dabney to the Governor of Fayal, our Minister at Rio Janeiro, and our Secretary of State. These letters will develop more fully the circumstances of this unfortunate affair.

We expect to sail tomorrow in a Portuguese brig for Amelia Island, which takes the whole of our crew; till when, I remain gentlemen, your very obedient humble servant.

***

CAPTAIN REID AFTERWARD

Captain Reid left Fayal in a Portuguese brig and arrived at Amelia Island with his officers and crew on the fifteenth of November 1814. They sailed via Amelia Island to Savannah where he and his men were feted for their exploits.

Reid continued to receive such ovations as he traveled from Savannah to New York where the New York Legislature presented him with an engraved sword.

The honors his exploits and those of his crew received were well deserved. But it was more than that. Much of the news concerning the war as far as most Americans were concerned had not been good. The American public was open and very anxious to receive good news reflecting the progress of the war and here was a magnificent David and Goliath story. The *General Armstrong* story quickly became a widely known subject of illustration, poetry, and song.

Reid went on to serve his country in another unusual way. In January 1817, Reid was asked by Representative Peter H. Wendover for advice in the design of a new U.S. flag. Representative Wendover was the head of a congressional committee tasked to design a new flag that reflected the countries brief history as well as making note of the new states joining the union.

The flag in use at the time had fifteen stars and fifteen stripes, and had not been updated since 1795. Five new states had joined the union since and it appeared likely that more would be joining in the near future. Any new flag design must be able to keep abreast of the new states.

Working together, Representative Wendover and Reid decided on a design that kept the number of stripes limited to the original thirteen, but placed twenty stars on the canton with the option of adding a new star each time a new state joined the union.

A Naval Incident at Horta

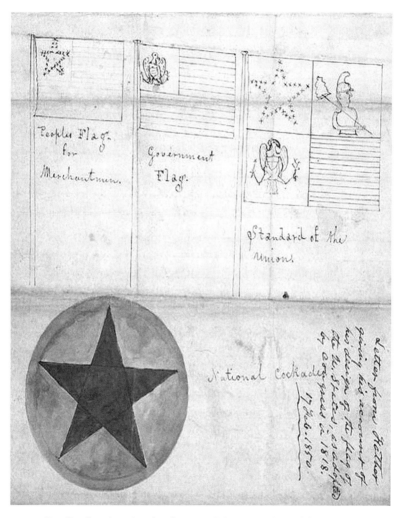

Reid's sketches for the design of the new Flag of the United States that he sent his son. The far left design was the one finally adopted. The canton was later changed from Reid's "great star" design to four rows of five stars each.

Reid actually sketched three flag designs, one for general use with the twenty stars arranged in the shape of a larger star; one for use on government vessels and buildings that featured an eagle on the canton instead of stars; and one for use on ceremonial occasions that featured a different element (stars, stripes, the Great Seal, and the Goddess of Liberty) on each of the flag's four quarters.

The congressional committee adopted Reid's general-use flag, but not his other two designs. Wendover drafted a bill asking that the thirteen-stripe, twenty-star design become the official flag of the United States. The bill was signed into law as the Flag Act of 1818 by President James Monroe on 4 April 1818.

Reid was productive in civil matters in other ways. In 1821 he invented and erected the first marine telegraph between Staten Island and the New York City Battery.

Through his efforts and instigation he caused the government to establish a lightship off Sandy Hook, the first ever constructed. (As a young seaman at the helm of a navy destroyer, at night in heavy weather, I went by the lightship moored to that station in 1948. It did not appear to be pleasant duty, with the waves sweeping over her deck and the whole ship lying heavy on one side. But on that night, in that weather, its strategic role as a navigation aide in that spot was unmistakable.)

Reid was appointed master in the Navy in 1844 and died in New York on 28 January 1861.

A Naval Incident at Horta

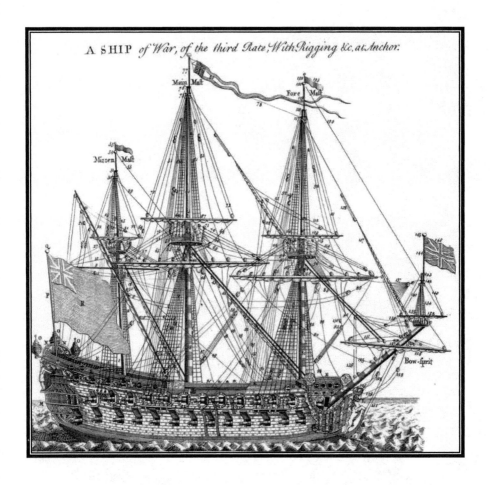

A Ship of War, of the Third Rate
(From Cyclopaedia, *Volume 2, 1728)*

Appendix B:

COMMODORE LLOYD'S REPORT TO REAR ADMIRAL BROWN AND COMMODORE LLOYD AND COMMANDER BENTHAM AFTERWARD

Robert Lloyd to William Brown

His Majesty's Ship *Plantagenet* Fayal Roads 28th September 1814

Sir,

I beg leave to inform you, that on the Evening of the 26th instant, I put into this port for refreshments, previous to my return to Jamaica. In shore was discovered a Suspicious Vessel at Anchor, I ordered Captain Bentham of the *Carnation* to watch her movements, and sent the pinnace and Cutter of this ship to assist him on that service, but on his perceiving her under weigh, he sent Lieut. Taufact in the pinnace to observe her proceedings.

On his approaching the Schooner, he was ordered to keep off or they would fire into him, upon which the boat was immediately backed off, but to his astonishment he received a broadside of round, grape and musquetry, which did considerable damage; he then requested them repeatedly to leave off firing, as he was not come to molest them, but the enemy still continued his destructive fire until they had killed two, and wounded seven men, without a musquet being returned by the Boat.

The conduct, in violating the neutrality of this Port, I conceived, left me no alternative but that of destroying her. I therefore repeatedly ordered Captain Bentham to tow the Brig in, and take that step immediately.

All the Boats of this ship and the *Rota*, were sent under his orders to tow alongside or assist in the attack as circumstances might require, but from continued light baffling winds and a lee tide, he was not able as he informed me with his utmost exertions, to put my orders in to execution, which I now most sincerely lament.

Finding the Privateer was warping under the forts very fast, Captain Bentham judged it prudent to lose no time, and about 12 ordered the Boats to make the attack.

A more gallant and determined one never was made, led on by Lieutenant Matterface of His Majesty's Ship *Rota*, & Downbank of this ship and every officer and man displayed the greatest courage in face of a heavy discharge of great guns & musquets.

But from her side being on the rocks, (which was not known at the time) and every American in Fayal exclusive of part of the crew, being armed & concealed in these rocks, which were immediately over the Privateer, it unfortunately happened when these boarding men gained the deck, they were under the painful necessity of returning to their Boats, from the very destructive fire kept up by those above them, from the shore, who were in complete security, and I am grieved to say not before many lives were lost, exclusive of the wounded.

Never were there any officers or men that behaved with more bravery, coolness resolution, &, as heroes, they are to be lamented as a great loss, to their King, their Country, and their friends.

Sometime after a favorable breeze sprung up, and Capt. Bentham soon anchored the brig close to the Privateer, and in a short time she was a perfect wreck & then burnt.

She proved to be the noted American Privateer *General Armstrong* pierced for 18, but mounting only Eight long 9's and one long 42 pr. Guns, about 360 Tons burthen, with a complement of 90 men, out 16 days from New York, had taken nothing, fitted out and bound on nine months cruise, one of the fastest sailing vessels out of America, & is said to have taken & destroyed British property to the amount of a million Dollars on her former cruises.

I am happy to say the *Carnation* had not a man hurt, altho' the Privateer kept up a brisk fire on her approach, when the Brig could not get a gun to bear.

Painful as it is to my feelings to announce the loss of so many brave men, I beg leave to enclose a list of the killed & wounded on board the Ship, I have the honor to command, as well as those of His Majesty's Ship *Rota*.

I sincerely hope that my Lords Commissioners of the Admiralty as well as yourself will be satisfied with my conduct, under the circumstances of so many of my brave crew being murdered in the most flagrant manner without the shadow of a pretence, by the Privateer firing on them in a neutral port, and when the conduct on the part of my Boats did not evince any thing like hostility.

For your further information, I beg leave to transmit you, a Copy of my letter to Capt. Bentham with his answer, as well as of the Governor of Royals letters to me with my answers thereto.

The Americans had endeavored according to their custom, to impress upon him a belief that it was the Boat that first commenced hostilities.

He has since informed the British Consul, that had he known the real circumstances of the case, he would in the event of the Privateer's being refused to be surrendered have ordered the Guns of the Fort to be opened on her, to assist the Boats in the Attack.

I am informed by Capt. Read of His Majesty's Sloop *Calypso*, that the *Grampus* American privateer in July last broke the neutrality of by destroying the [sic] Transport while at anchor off that place.

I have the honor &c ...

Lloyd Captain

William Brown

COMMODORE LLOYD AND COMMANDER BENTHAM AFTERWARD

Commodore Lloyd and *Plantagenet* did finally arrive at Jamaica in time to join Admiral Cochrane's ill-fated invasion fleet. After the land battle of 8 January 1815, *Plantagenet* was given the dubious honor of taking the bodies of Generals Pakenham and Gibbs back to England.

Lloyd remained as captain of *Plantagenet* until April 1815 (the *Plantagenet* was broken up in 1817). Although Lloyd received no further command, he remained on half pay and continued to accrue seniority, becoming a Rear Admiral in July 1830 and finally Vice Admiral in January 1837.

He died in January 1846.

Commander Bentham did make Post-Captain. Although it is not clear whether *Carnation* under his command accompanied Lloyd with the invasion fleet to take New Orleans (I say this as *Rota*, under Post-Captain Philip Somerville's command, did not.)

Bentham was in Port Royal when the dockyard caught fire. His work in saving it from destruction gained him strong recommendations that precipitated his being made Acting-Captain to the *North Star* on 29 November 1815, and 6 July 1816, to the *Heron*.

In consideration of his services in the latter vessel at the Battle of Algiers, Commander Bentham was rewarded by advancement to Post-rank, 16 September, 1816.

He retired on 1 October 1846.

Paul Estronza La Violette

The Portugese Forte de Santa Cruz (very much exaggerated) from whose ramparts many of the local citizenry such as the british observer in this Appedix watched the several naval actions in the Bay of Horta.

(Detail of the Nathaniel Currier print of the second action shown on pages 120-121)

Appendix C:

LETTER FROM A BRITISH OBSERVER ASHORE *

Fayal, Oct 15, 1814.

  Wm. Cobbett, Esq. — Sir, the American Brig privateer *General Armstrong*, of New York, Captain Samuel C. Reid, of seven guns and ninety men, entered here on the 26th ult. about noon, seventeen days from that place, for the purpose of obtaining water.

  The Captain seeing nothing on the horizon, was induced to anchor. Before the elapse of many hours, his Majesty's brig *Carnation* came in and anchored near her. About six his Majesty's ship *Plantagenet*, of seventy-four guns, and the *Rota* frigate, came in and anchored also.

  The Captain of the privateer and his friends consulted the authorities here about her security. They all considered her perfectly secure, and that his Majesty's officers were too well acquainted with the respect due to a neutral port to molest her. But to the great surprise of every one, about nine in the evening, four boats were dispatched, armed and manned from his Majesty's ships, for the purpose of cutting her out.

---

*Published in *Cobbett's Weekly Register*, 10 December 1814

It being about full of moon, the night perfectly clear and calm, we could see every movement made. The boats approached with rapidity towards her, when, it appears the Captain of the privateer hailed them, and told them to keep off several times.

They, notwithstanding, pushed on, and were in the act of boarding before any defense was made for the privateer. A warm contest ensued on both sides. The boats were finally dispersed with great loss.

The American, now calculating on a very superior force being sent, cut his cables, and rowed the privateer close in along side of the fort, within half cable's length, where he moored her, head and stem, with four lines.

The Governor now sent a remonstrance to the Van Lloyd of the *Plantagenet* against such proceedings, and trusted that the privateer would not be further molested; she being in the dominions of Portugal, and under the guns of the castle, "was entitled to Portuguese protection."

Van Lloyd's answer was that he was determined to destroy the vessel at the expense of all Fayal, and should any protection be given her by the fort, he would not leave a house standing in the village.

All the inhabitants were gathered about the walk, expecting a renewal of the attack. At midnight, fourteen launches were discovered to be coming in rotation for the purpose. When they got within range of gun shot, a tremendous and effectual discharge was made from the privateer which threw the boats into confusion.

They now returned a spirited fire, but the privateer kept up so continual a discharge, it was almost impossible for the boats to make any progress.

They finally succeeded, after immense loss, to get along side of her, and attempted to board at every quarter, cheered by the officers with a shout of no quarters, which we could distinctly hear, as well as their shrieks and cries.

The termination was near about a total massacre. Three of the boats were sunk, and but one poor solitary officer escaped death in a boat that contained fifty souls, he was wounded.

The Americans fought with great firmness. Some of the boats were left without a single man to row them; others with three and four. The most that any one returned with was about ten. Several boats floated on shore full of dead bodies.

With great reluctance I state that they were manned with picked men, and commanded by the first, second, third, and fourth Lieutenants of the *Plantagenet*; first, second, third, and fourth ditto of the frigate, and the first officers of the brig; together with a great number of midshipmen.

Our whole force exceeded four hundred men. But three officers escaped, two of which are wounded. This bloody and unfortunate contest lasted about forty minutes.

After the boats gave out, nothing more was attempted till daylight the next morning, when the *Carnation* hauled in along side, and engaged her. The privateer still continued to make a most gallant defense. These veterans reminded all of Lawrence's words of the *Chesapeake*, "don't give up the ship."

The *Carnation* lost one of her top masts, and her yards were shot away; she was much cut up in rigging, and received several shot in her hull. This obliged her to haul off to repair, and to cease firing.

The Americans now finding their principal gun (Long Tom) and several others dismounted deemed it folly to think of saving her against such a superior force. They therefore cut away her masts to the deck. Blew a few through her bottom, took out their small arms, clothing, &c. and went on shore.

I discovered only two shot holes in the hull of the privateer, although much cut up in rigging. Two boats' crews were soon after dispatched from our vessels, which went on board took some provisions and set her on fire.

For three days after, we were employed in burying the dead that washed on shore in the surf. The number of British killed exceeds one hundred and twenty, and ninety wounded. The enemy to the surprise of mankind, lost only two killed and seven wounded.

We may well say "God deliver us from our enemies, if this is the way the Americans fight."

After burning the privateer, Van Lloyd made a demand of the Governor to deliver up the Americans as his prisoners, which the Governor refused. He threatened to send five hundred men on shore and take them by force.

The Americans immediately retired, with their arms, to an old Gothic convent; knocked away the adjoining drawbridge, and determined to defend themselves to the last. The Van, (sic) however, thought better than to send his men. He then demanded two men, who, he said, deserted from his vessel when in America. The Governor sent for these men but found no one of that description

Many houses received much injury on shore from the guns of the *Carnation*. A woman sitting in the fourth story of her house had her thigh shot off, and a boy had his arm broken.

The American Consul here has made a demand on the Portuguese government for a hundred thousand dollars for the privateer, which our consul, Mr. Parkin, thinks in justice will be paid, and that they will claim on England. Mr. Parkin, Mr. Edward Bayley, and other English gentlemen, disapprove of the outrage and depredation committed by our vessels on this occasion.

The vessel that was dispatched to England with the wounded was not permitted to take a single letter from any person. Being an eye-witness to this transaction, I have given you a correct statement as it occurred.

With respect, I am, etc.

H. K. F.

A Naval Incident at Horta

Paul Estronza La Violette

*The Battle of New Orleans, by Dennis M. Carter 1856
(Williams Research Center of The Historic New Orleans
Collection)*

Appendix D:

DID THE BATTLE OF FAYAL REALLY LEAD TO THE BATTLE OF NEW ORLEANS?

*A*t the start of this book, I mention the problem I had in separating the major participants' self-promotion from true accounts of the happenings in Horta in September 1814. Despite this problem, I think this book presents as accurate a story of the battle between the *General Armstrong* and the British squadron as the data available allows.

However, it is what is reported to have happened as a result of the battle with which I still have problems. Probably the one sentence or phrase that epitomizes my difficulty is the remark that many attribute to General Andrew Jackson:

"*If it weren't for the Battle of Fayal, there wouldn't have been a Battle of New Orleans.*"

Nowhere, in any of the sources I used for this book, have I found where or when Jackson is supposed to have made this rather curious remark. I say curious, because Jackson was well aware of the events that led up to the Battle of New

Orleans and, as a result, I find it difficult to believe he would make such a remark.

My opinion aside, the question remains: did the Battle of Fayal really lead to the Battle of New Orleans? There are a number of reliable sources that discuss the Battle of Fayal that believe it did. Their argument seems to revolve around four principal points.

1. Lloyd was ordered to report in all haste to Admiral Cochran in Negril Bay, Jamaica.
2. Lloyd was late in arriving at Jamaica. His late arrival threw the invasion's tight schedule into such disarray that the invasion was delayed for several critical weeks.
3. Lloyd's squadron carried needed supplies (i.e., troops, transport barges, etc.) for the upcoming British invasion.
4. Lloyd's squadron of three ships was an important, perhaps even key, segment of the armada that was to form the invasion fleet.

Let us examine the first point. The following letter addressed to the Admiralty Board's First Secretary, John W. Croker accompanied *Thais* back to Great Britain. It is rather informative.

>Robert Lloyd to John W. Croker
>His Majesty's Ship *Plantagenet*
>3rd October 1814,
>Fayal Roads, Azores
>   Sir,
>
>"... I beg leave to acquaint you for the information of my Lords Commissioners of the Admiralty. That I was not able on the 1st. Instant, from the bad state of the weather, to get any more, that the wounded of this Ship, on board the

Calypso, which I ordered immediately to proceed with my dispatch for their Lordships information.
 Yesterday a heavy gale of wind coming on I was obliged to put to sea, but the weather having moderated, I again returned here this morning, & hope to get the *Rota's* wounded on board the *Thais*, so that she will be able to sail in the evening or early tomorrow morning.
 ... *I shall proceed with His Majesty's ships under my command, with further execution of Rear Admiral Brown's (orders?) but in hopes of being able to destroy some of the Enemy's numerous Privateers, shall take a northerly route, so far as the Longitude of 30^000 West, before I make (sic) right course to – Jamaica, which I hope the Lordships as well as the Rear Admiral will approve of...."*

 Consider this last paragraph in Lloyd's letter (the italicizes in the original letter are mine). Why, as it states, would he wander into the broad Atlantic looking for *the Enemy's numerous Privateers* if he had been ordered to proceed at all haste to Jamaica?
 The second point concerns Jamaica. Admiral Cochrane had set up the planning for the invasion of the southern United States months earlier. The invasion fleet was scheduled to gather in Negril Bay, Jamaica no later than 20 November. This was a firm date known to all the major participants in the operation.
 Commodore Lloyd certainly knew of it. According to *Plantagenet's* log, he showed up in Negril Bay with all three ships of the squadron on 13 November; almost a week ahead of schedule.
 Rather than late, Lloyd was early - a week early!
 It also appears from the above letter that he was under Admiral Brown's West Indies command. It appears his squadron was not engaged in carrying men or supplies to Jamaica, but rather was under orders from Admiral Brown to

cruise the Atlantic and look, as he states in this letter, for *the Enemy's numerous Privateers.*

Vice Admiral Sir Alexander Cochrane, National Portrait Gallery. Engraving by Charles Turner (1774–1857) after a painting by William Beechey (1753–1839)

General Andrew Jackson. (Courtesy The Mariners' Museum Newport News Naval Archives)

As to the third point, there were no extra troops or barges aboard the squadron's vessels. The men and launches used to attack *General Armstrong* were all taken from the normal complement of men and boats such a group of warships carries for operations such as they attempted at Horta.

There certainly was not a surplus of men and boats; the midnight action all but depleted the squadron's supply of both. In fact, Lloyd was forced to commandeer men from *Calypso* and *Thais* to replenish those in the squadron killed or wounded in the fighting.

The forth point is baffling on the face of it.

Think about it. Think about the immensity of the planned invasion and then think of Lloyd's small, three-ship squadron. Admiral Cochrane was assembling an armada of some sixty-five vessels, most of these major warships, including a number of ships-of-the-line. They carried more than 10,000 British troops!!! How could a small, three-ship squadron make a difference that would affect the success of such an armada?

I believe the events that occurred during the initiation and actual invasion are what motivated Admiral Cochrane's decision of where and when he would invade and these decisions had nothing to do with the "late" presence of Lloyd's squadron.

From the very start of the New Orleans campaign, Cochrane had the choice of three avenues on which to invade. One of these was to gain control of Mobile via Mobile Bay.

Cochrane preferred this avenue of attack. Once Mobile was captured, he would use it as an operational base from which to pivot the army westward and, with a 140-mile overland march, attack New Orleans via Lake Pontchartrain.

Admiral Cochrane felt this would be a fairly standard military operation; one the army had shown to be quite successful in conducting in Europe. Perhaps this route's major fault was that it was predictable and, as it turned out, General Jackson had no trouble predicting it.

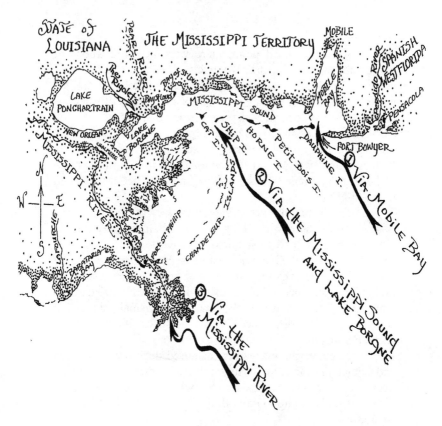

The Three Possible British Invasion Routes
(From Sink or Be Sunk*)*

    The second approach was through the shallow waters of the broad estuaries (now called the Mississippi Sound and Lake Borgne) lying behind the coastal barrier of islands.
    It was an approach whose main fault was that it was physically demanding. It would mean rowing barges loaded with troops and their equipment some eighty miles thus putting an arduous strain on the invasion troops before they even arrived to do battle with Jackson at New Orleans.

A Naval Incident at Horta

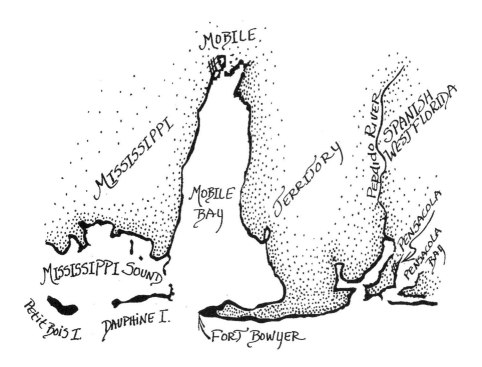

*The Battle areas for Mobile
(From* Sink or Be Sunk*)*

The third approach, and the one he wanted the least to attempt, was to engage in a long, upstream struggle up the Mississippi River. This actually was attempted in January 1815, but proved as futile as originally thought.

So Admiral Cochrane tried the first approach, the capture of Mobile. He launched a combined land and sea attack in mid-September against Fort Bowyer at the entrance to Mobile Bay. At the same time, he attempted to set up a base of supply and operations in Spanish-ruled Pensacola.

However, in a series of brilliant moves, General Andrew Jackson checkmated him in a humiliating way at Fort Bowyer and, immediately after, did the same at Pensacola. Jackson then made a mistake; he stayed in Mobile, expecting the British to try another attack.

When Cochrane became aware of this, he realized he had a narrow window of opportunity.

He quickly shifted the invasion force into position to use the second invasion route, i.e., through the shallow waters of the Mississippi Sound and Lake Borgne.

Cochrane felt that once Jackson realized his mistake and raced to New Orleans, he would be unable to organize the city's defenses before British troops began their major assault.

Events proved Cochrane wrong, but that's another story. The important thing here is that the preceding events are what set up the timing and placement of Cochrane's invasion anchorage off the coast of what is now Mississippi.

Lloyd's stop at Horta and the resulting naval action involving the *General Armstrong* had nothing to do with it.

A Naval Incident at Horta

Glossary

Admiral The highest rank of naval officer. Subdivided into three ranks, with Admiral being highest, Vice Admiral, middle rank, and Rear Admiral being lowest. Each of these, in the early 18th-century British navy, was further subdivided into three colors denoting rank: red highest, white middle, and blue lowest.

Admiralty Board The administrative board superintending the early 18th-century British navy. The executive officer of the board was the First Secretary.

anchor cable The strong, thick rope attached to an anchor.

block A wooden pulley or combination of wooden pulleys used to increase the power of the ropes running through it. Used to hoist heavy rigging.

blunderbuss A short barreled gun with a large bore and wide mouth.

boarding pike A sharp pointed spike at the end of a long staff used in boarding an enemy vessel.

boatswain An all-purpose, experienced petty officer, usually in charge of sails and rigging.

bow chaser A long cannon placed in a bow port to fire at a chase, or vessel, directly ahead.

bowsprit A large spar running from the stem (or bow timber) from which foremast stays are attached and jibs are set.

brig A two-masted sailing boat, square rigged on both masts.

Brigantine A two-masted sailing boat, square rigged except for a fore-and-aft mainsail.

Broadside The simultaneous firing of the guns on one side of a vessel.

Cable A strong, thick rope.

canister also **canister shot** or **case-shot** A thin cylinder containing small iron balls.

carronade A short barreled, comparatively light, gun capable of firing a heavy charge a short distance.

Chain shot Two solid balls connected by chain fired from cannon primarily at an enemy's masts, sails, or rigging. Sometimes used to clear an enemy deck before boarding.

Commodore A post-captain appointed to temporarily command a pro tem squadron of warships. Authorized to fly a swallow-tailed pennant while holding the temporary rank and considered the first rank of flag rank officers.

Con Steer a ship.

Consul The representative of a country residing in a foreign country representing the interests of the appointing country.

Coup de main A sudden attack by force. In nautical terms, usually a cutting out of an enemy vessel in a harbor by small boats.

coxswain The helmsman of a ship's boat.

Cutlass A short, curving sword used by sailors.

Figurehead The carved figure on a ship's bow.

First Lieutenant The senior lieutenant on a ship, usually the second in Command, often referred to as "First".

flagship A ship bearing an admiral's or commodore's flag.

foretop A small platform at the top of the foremast, below the fore topmast. Used as marine sharpshooters' platform in battle.

frigate A three-masted, fully rigged ship carrying twenty to fifty guns on the main deck and having a raised quarterdeck and forecastle.

gallery A beam-wide balcony, usually ornately carved, built outside the body of a ship on the stern.

gig A light boat, usually used exclusively for the captain of a vessel and tended by his coxswain.

grape or grapeshot Small iron balls bound in a bag that, when fired from a cannon, spread like shotgun pellets.

grapnel An iron-clawed hook on a line used to hook onto an enemy ship while boarding. Also used as an anchor over uneven bottoms.

harbor pilot A skilled, knowledgeable pilot of a port who is entrusted to bring ships safely into an anchorage.

harbormaster An officer of the port who controls the regulations pertaining to ships entering or leaving a port.

head money A reward for prisoners taken in battle.

hull The shell of a ship. When hit hard enough to crack or pierce, the expression is "to hull".

langrage A loss bundle of extremely jagged material fired at an enemy's rigging and sails or at deck height prior to boarding.

launches The largest boats carried by a man-of-war. Capable of carrying a carronade in the bow.

letter of marque A certificate carried by a private armed vessel allowing it to seize and take possession of an enemy's merchant vessels for its own use or gain.

London Gazette The official government journal listing government appointments, promotions, and other public notices.

long gun A cannon as opposed to a carronade.

marine A specialized soldier, as opposed to a sailor, who carried out soldier-type duties aboard a man-of-war.

master An officer with the same rank as lieutenant, but subordinate to him. Responsible for the navigation and sailing of a vessel.

mast A vertical pole to support a vessel's sails. Normally reaches below deck to the keel.

midshipman A candidate ship officer.

mole A massive earthen or stone pier projecting out in the water in such a fashion as to provide sheltered landing places for boats.

netting Large gauge netting used to prevent boarders' access to a vessel and when spread horizontally over gun decks, to catch falling spars, blocks, and riggings.

North American Station In the parlance of the late 17th- and 18th-century British navy, the duty station encompassing Canada and the United States.

parapet The wall in front of the foot platform of a fort.

parole A promise of a prisoner of war to not try to escape if released under his own supervision or loose supervision.

pinnace A narrow boat, usually with eight oars.

port The left side of a vessel facing forward.

port quarter The left after portion of a vessel facing forward.

Post-Captain The permanent naval rank above commander and below admiral.

powder monkey The person bringing up the powder from the vessel's magazine to the guns, usually a child of twelve or slightly older.

42 or xx pounder A cannon or carronade that fires a certain weight ball.

press A method by which the British navy enrolled by force civilians or sometimes foreign seamen into serving in the navy.

Privateer A private armed vessel carrying a *Letter of Marque* from a government, allowing it to seize and take possession of an enemy's merchant vessels for its own use or gain.

Prize A captured enemy vessel and its cargo.

Prize money The profits accrued from the sale of a prize.

Quarter Mercy or clemency toward a stricken opponent.

'Quasi-War' The war between the United States and France during the period 1798-1800.

raked masts The slant of a vessel's masts to increase speed.

razee A ship-of-the-line reduced in height by removing her upper deck, making her lighter.

schooner A fore-and-aft-rigged vessel.

Second Lieutenant A naval officer holding a lieutenant's commission, but subordinate to the vessel's first lieutenant and normally in line for becoming first. A lesser commissioned officer would be the vessel's third lieutenant.

shrouds Lines that support the masts and extend from the mast to the sides of the ship.

sloop A small sailing vessel.

spars The general term for all the horizontal poles in a vessel's riggings.

spring A line made fast to one end of an anchor cable and at the other end to the ship's after quarter. By hauling on it, the vessel is brought broadside to the anchor.

square-rigged A vessel with sails set across the masts as opposed to fore and aft.

standing in Entering a port.

starboard The right side of a vessel facing forward.

swallow-tailed pennant A broad pennant carried by a commodore.

sweeps Long oars used to maneuver or tow a vessel.

swivel gun A small portable cannon resting in a swivel mounted to a ship's rail.

tidal current The current set up by the rise and fall of the tide. Maximum flow occurs between high and low tide.

Vice Consul A consul officer subordinate to a consul.

weather gauge A position in a vessel engagement where one vessel is upwind of the other vessel, thus being able to maneuver to the better advantage.

weigh anchor Lift the vessel's anchor.

A Naval Incident at Horta

The title page of the memoirs of the Horta Battle as written in 1893 by Captain Samuel Chester Reid's son, Sam Reid. *(Library of Congress)*

The title page of the Annals of the Dabney Family in Fayal *written in 1900 by John Bass Dabney's granddaughter, Roxana Lewis Dabney.* (Boston, for private circulation, ca. 1899).

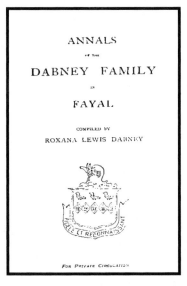

Acknowledgements

There are a number of sources I have used for this book. Most were excellent and provided me information I would not have obtained by any other means.

One of these is the 1893 book by Captain Reid's son, Samuel Reid: *The Wonderful Battle of the Brig* General Armstrong *at Fayal, Azores 1814*. Although naturally biased in favor of his father, it is a gathering of details that pretty much tells what happened almost two hundred years ago. I have used a number of his illustrations in this book. For my purposes, the most important of his illustrations was the anchor motif on his cover. I have used it to mark the end of each of the chapters in this book.

Another equally informative account can be found in the *Annals of the Dabney Family* compiled by Roxana (Roxie) Lewis Dabney, 1827-1913, daughter of Charles William Dabney, and granddaughter of Consul John Bass Dabney.

Both books suffer somewhat from the fact that neither of the authors were first-hand witnesses to the Horta actions, but each includes reports written by people who were present. Captain Reid's final report is in Samuel Reid's account, and John Dabney's report and correspondence are in Roxana Dabney's *Annals*.

Except for ship and captain logs (which I will discuss later in this acknowledgement), I do not have this same luxury in finding first-hand accounts of the British side of the battle.

In fact, except for the report by Commander George Bentham of his limited involvement in the second of the night actions of *Carnation*, I found nothing more authoritative than the final report of Commodore Robert Lloyd. This, unfortunately, for both its briefness and at times incredible deviation from what all other evidence indicates actually occurred, is the entire British case.

Much of this scarcity of British accounts is the result of the tight censor Lloyd made of the battle and the fact that the far more important Battle of New Orleans followed close to the Horta incident. In writing of the naval skirmishes concerning New Orleans, I found a number of British personal accounts that helped give me an accurate version of the New Orlean's actions than the stifled, one-sided story permitted by Lloyd of the Horta events.

There is the later British report of the Horta action by Admiral William James in his 1837 *Naval History of Great Britain* – Vol. VI. In his report concerning Horta, James merely parrots Lloyd's short account, including several of Lloyd's misstatements. Theodore Roosevelt's account in his 1882 book, *The Naval War of 1812,* is too brief to add much information beyond placing it in perspective to what was going on in other areas of the war.

However, I did find voluminous sources of very useful, data in the American and British archival records. The first of these data sets was found through the kind assistance of the researchers in the Navy History and Heritage Command (US). Their work in searching the archives disclosed among other bits of what initially seemed trivia, a number of Lloyd's letters, as well as transcripts of correspondence from the British Admiralty Board to Commodore Lloyd. To my personal pleasure, I found in their exhibit hall the 42-pounder, Long Tom, and the *General Armstrong's* figurehead. Pictures of both can be found elsewhere in this book.

In all my research, Commodore Robert Lloyd was my biggest puzzle. The bare bones depiction of his career in *A Naval Biographical Dictionary* compiled in 1849 by William R. O'Bryne, is certainly unfulfilling. From this I learned of his naval career prior to Horta; a career in which Lloyd seems to have been a quite capable, if rather aggressive, British naval officer.

But when I compare these earlier actions with his strange and at times overbearing actions at Horta, this same aggressiveness seems almost unbalanced. My problem is I cannot find anything personal about Lloyd before or during the Horta actions, or for that matter afterward, that tell me anything about the man himself beyond the fact that he was ashore without a ship six month later. But this may have been because of the British/American war being over.

To flesh out my narrative, I have occasionally indulged in a bit of storytelling in some of the actions (but remaining as close to what was said to have occurred as possible). I feel somewhat embarrassed by this in relating what was said between Commodore Lloyd and his First in Chapter 2, but in truth, I feel that what I wrote was in spirit if not in actuality, was how he might well have behaved.

Unfortunately, this leaves me with a narration of the Horta actions that, by the limitation of its data sources, is heavily biased toward the American viewpoint, but I have no choice.

As to the relevance all this has to the Battle of New Orleans, I make my case concerning this in Appendix D. It is up to the reader to decide. The trouble, of course, is that the claim by many that the Battle of Fayal and the Battle of New Orleans are irrecusably tied raises what happened in the Port of Horta in September 1814, to another level in American history. It has been acclaimed to be one of those great happenings like Bunker Hill, the Battle of the Alamo, and the Battle of the Bulge.

Maybe, maybe not. But let me repeat what I said in Chapter 7 about Reid and his men's decision to fight:

What was unusual about this was that Reid and his men did not have to continue their fight: they had nothing to gain by continuing.

Honor, if that was what was wanted, was already theirs. By all accounts, they had made a superb stand against a vastly superior force. There would be no dishonor in setting fire to the vessel and retreating into the town.

Apparently Reid did not want to do this, and, as he walked and talked with the waiting men, it seemed that most did not want to do this as well.

Paul Estronza La Violette

I contend there is greatness in acts of defiant courage that by these acts alone raises the person(s) involved to great heights. It is these acts by Captain Reid and his men that this book is about.

I would like to end my acknowledgments in citing several people whose invaluable involvement in this book is scattered over a great many pages.

Most prominent of these is Consul Gavin A. Sundwall and his staff at the American Consulate in Ponta Delgada, Azores. He and his staff gave my wife, Stella, and I personal service while we were in the Azores that would have been impossible to duplicate if we would have tried to do so on our own.

In addition to library and university sources in Ponta Delgada, Consul Sundwall introduced us to American expatriates Paula and Tim Colwell, who gave us similarly wonderful help in Fayal's library and universities, as well as Horta's municipal's archives. Both Consul Sundwall and these two wonderful people opened doors to us that we would never have known existed.

Lastly, another rich and basic data source was provided by Jose Vetta Wise and his son, Jonathan, who spent hours poring through a maze of National Archives in London, England. Their diligent search was rewarded with many valuable sources that were beyond my reach, and I have included in many pages of this book.

Among the informative data they provided, I am chiefly indebted for the ships' and captains' logs of the three British vessels that took part in the Horta actions. Certainly, without these logs, reliable knowledge of the critical actions of *Carnation* would not have been possible. So I would like to close this account with my particular thanks and gratitude to these two wonderfully kind people.

A Naval Incident at Horta

The ship's log of HMS Calypso *(National Archives, England). The author is indebted for this picture and the log entries of the British warships to Jose Vetta Wise and his son, Jonathan.*

Paul Estronza La Violette

ABOUT THE AUTHOR

Paul Estronza La Violette has engaged in basic marine research aboard research ships and aircraft in most of the world's oceans, most especially in the Arctic and the Mediterranean. His scientific publications include ocean atlases, as well as books and papers on the circulation of the world's oceans and seas.

His first nonscientific book, Views from a Front Porch, *published in 1999, was sold out in slightly less than a year. Its success prompted he and his wife, Stella, to form a two-person company, Annabelle Books, to publish their books. Since its inception, he has written nine other books that have continued the success of his first book. These may be ordered through their web site: www.annabellebooks.com.*

The books presently in print that may be ordered via Annabelle Books are:
Sink or Be Sunk
Holly! and his Black Coat of Invisibility
One Dog, Two Dogs, Three Dogs, Four…
A White Egret In The Shallows
Blueberry Peaches, Red Robin Pie
The Way to Stone Hill

Paul Estronza La Violette